Illustrations reprinted courtesy of the Free Library of Philadelphia.
Designed by Jeannette Jacobs

First published in the United States of America in 1976 by the Walker Publishing Company, Inc.

Published simultaneously in Canada by Fitzhenry & Whiteside, Limited, Toronto.

Trade ISBN: 0-8027-6251-4
Reinf. ISBN; 0-8027-6252-2

Library of Congress Catalog Card Number: 75-43990

Printed in the United States of America.

10 9 8 7 6 5 4 3 2 1

To the memory of
Mother, Edna, and Pat

". . . The world is all so changed;
so much that seemed vigorous has sunk decrepit,
so much that was not is beginning to be!—
Borne over the Atlantic, to the closing ear of Louis,
King by the Grace of God, what sounds are these;
muffled-ominous, new in our centuries?
Boston Harbour is black with unexpected Tea;
behold a Pennsylvanian Congress gather;
and ere long, on Bunker Hill, DEMOCRACY
announcing, in rifle-volleys death-winged,
under her Star Banner, to the tune of Yankee-doodle-doo,
that she is born, and, whirlwind-like,
will envelop the world!"

—Thomas Carlyle, *The French Revolution*

CONTENTS

PREFACE

Time has a way of altering viewpoints of fateful changes in the world and of cloaking them with a sentimental mist; but in all history the American Revolution and the French Revolution remain irrevocably linked. For America's brave blow for liberty was the winged spark from afar destined to ignite the smoldering fire of revolution in France, her eventual triumph over oppression, the wind that served to fan the flame.

Even before the word "Independence" rang out loud and clear, the eyes of the American Congress had turned toward Europe for support: financial aid, a steady flow of supplies, and a fleet to offset Britain's control of the seas. The question was, Who would risk an open break with powerful England?

As early as November, 1775, when venerable and persuasive Benjamin Franklin had been sent to Europe to "feel out" foreign aid, supplies were being shipped from

France to America in secret. These were to be followed later by adventuresome Frenchmen (notably the young Marquis de La Fayette) eager to fight alongside the Americans and enthused by the dream of equality and justice, a goal they too hoped to achieve.

The French Treaty of Alliance was signed by Franklin in France on February 6, 1778; it reached America and was ratified by Congress on May 2.

This was cause for celebration by both countries and by the French and American people who now shared a common aim. The king had been advised to sign this treaty of mutual agreement which assured France's cooperation in continued hostilities towards America's independence. America, in return, guaranteed defense of the French West Indies in the case of war between France and England, seemingly a certainty.

With the words, "Firmly assure the Congress of my friendship. I hope this will be for the good of both nations," falling from the lips of King Louis XVI during the most crucial period of the American Revolution, the kinship of the two countries was sealed. These words also helped to seal the fate of one of the most unfortunate kings in history.

History comes down to us from the distillation of materials: documentation gives us facts and figures; fiction, or a writer's imagination, colors documentation with emotion. This story is a combination of both.

Many have written their versions of the French Revolution, that most terrible and in some ways most worthy period in history. The National Archives of France, the reportage of people who were there, the writings of loyal courtiers and vindictive enemies—all have filtered down to us a wide and varied interpretation of that bloodthirsty event. For, like spectators at some accident or catastrophe, each observer seems to see it differently.

But surely the *intimates* of the royal family of France, those who resided with them through both happy and tragic days, must be considered the most trustworthy. It is from these, including Mme de Tourzel, faithful governess of the royal children, and Mme Campan, first lady-in-waiting to the queen, that much of this portrait has been drawn. This is how they saw it.

But most of all this is how Marie Thérèse Charlotte, called Madame Royale, teenage daughter of Louis XVI and Marie Antoinette, *lived* it—not with a gross simpleton for a father, as some historians have typified the king; not with a wicked and unfeeling mother, as the queen has so often been pictured; but with a man and woman subject to the faults and frailties common to all human beings, nevertheless possessed with goodness and character that were reflected in their children. Madame Royale recorded this in a journal she started while imprisoned in the Temple with her family. It was first published by M. de Saint-Amand (Firman Didot, Paris), date unknown. The original copy was given to the family of Francois Huë, a devoted attendant of the royal family. Major parts of this book were extracted from that journal. The marvel of her journal is that this heretofore sheltered young girl could write about the fearful cyclone whirling about her, and in which she and her family were the focal point, with the objective detachment of a reporter on the scene.

It is a fact that the French court was notoriously pleasure loving and irresponsible. But one must remember that this was a *teenage* court when the fourteen-year-old Marie Antoinette came to France to marry the not yet sixteen-year-old dauphin. His brothers were thirteen and fourteen. Small wonder that a time of restlessness and frivolity followed, a wild pursuit of entertainment and the fun of life. It is the story of youth. They were too young to realize the dangers.

But the manner in which this family—man, woman and child—bore the blows of bitter adversity and barbaric cruelty, and the gallant and even noble way they met their fate, is the glory of France.

INTRODUCTION: THE FRENCH REVOLUTION

The French Revolution, revolution of world importance, began in 1789 at a time when France was ruled by the privileged classes—the nobility and the clergy—who supplemented their funds by exacting ever-increasing dues from the lower classes, who bore all of the nation's financial burdens and reaped none of the benefits.

Among the peasant class a few serfs still existed, and there was a small group of landowners. However, most of the populace were tenant farmers subject to feudal taxes and tithes, to the avarice of royal agents, military service, and to other impositions, if not outright brutalities.

Recurrent famines, particularly of the staple grains, and freezing winters without adequate housing whipped the lower classes into a state of frenzy, aggravated by the wasteful luxury and corrupt living of the ruling classes. When, after generations of reigning dissolute kings, France was found to be on the verge of bankruptcy, the downtrodden people placed the blame not so much on their king, Louis XVI, a man of simple tastes, but on his Austrian-born queen, the youthfully frivolous and extravagant Marie Antoinette.

Economic reforms advocated by the king and his finance minister in a Convocation of Notables were thwarted by the refusal of the nobles and the clergy to sacrifice any of their privileges or to contribute to the country's welfare, and by the king's failure to provide strong support for the reforms. The Second Convocation of Notables was called in 1787 and, in the hope of avoiding mounting national debt and the ultimate bankruptcy of France, the nobles and clergy were asked to share in the taxes. Again they refused. Elections were ordered, and on May 5, 1789, for the first time in one hundred and sixty years, the States-General met at Versailles. Each of the three estates, or classes of society—Clergy, Nobles and Commons—was to present its particular grievances to the Crown, and Finance Minister Necker was to draw from this a general fiscal reform. But the steady stream of *cahiers* (list of grievances) pouring in from the provinces made it clear that political and social reforms much more radical than those that were likely to result from the meeting were expected.

The awakening Commons, the Third Estate, having had time to double its membership, now overbalanced the other two estates. Gathering strength, they declared that they, the Commons, *were* the nation. The question was raised as to whether the estates should meet separately and vote by order, or meet jointly and vote by head. The latter, of course, would assure a majority for the Third Estate because of its superior number.

The king was in a quandary, swayed first by this

opinion and then that. As he wavered, the deputies of the Third Estate took matters into their own hands and on June 17 proclaimed themselves the National Assembly; nevermore would they be known as the lowest, or Third Estate. They refused to adjourn (as had always been done at the king's bidding), and when the king ordered the assembly hall closed against them they moved to an indoor tennis court. There, on June 20, 1789, they took the famous "Oath of the Tennis Court," vowing to remain until a constitution had been recognized declaring the "rights of man."

On June 27 the king yielded and recognized the National Assembly. At the same time, he surrounded Versailles with troops and on July 11, urged by the queen who was intent on preserving the heritage of the throne for her son, dismissed and banished Finance Minister Necker. The people considered this finance minister their friend since he had been frank enough to publish a *Compte Rendu* (Account Rendered) revealing the sad state of governmental affairs in 1781. On July 14 they revolted and paraded in protest, carrying a plaster bust of Necker. The mob grew in numbers and in violence until, finally, thousands stormed the Bastille, the grim Paris jail, releasing prisoners and murdering the guards who stood in their way.

The king compromised by calling off his troops, and on July 17 going to Paris almost totally unattended to calm the people by indicating his recognition of their political power. He also recalled Necker and sanctioned the establishment of the Commune, which represented the interests of the people, as the new city government of Paris. The National Guard, "the people's army," was organized under the Marquis de La Fayette, a military man who had fought alongside George Washington in the American Revolution.

The insurrection of July was not limited to Paris. Mobilized by acute food shortages and economic depression, by the unfulfilled hopes aroused by the calling of the States-General, by fear of an aristocratic conspiracy; outraged by reports of royal scandals; and inflamed by revolutionary orators, the peasants threw off all restraint. The country areas were plagued with burning and looting, while labor troubles disrupted the city. On August 4 the nobles and clergy in the Assembly, driven partly by terror and partly by a burst of generosity, relinquished their privileges, abolishing in one night the traditional feudal structure of France. This act was followed by the drafting of the *Declaration of the Rights of Man and Citizen.*

Radical politics were gaining strength in Paris and rumors of counterrevolutionary plots and Court intrigues were circulated wildly. Spurred by the revolutionary rhetoric, the rumors of intrigue, and the king's resistance to the August innovations, a Parisian mob led by furious women marched on Versailles on October 5, 1789. The royal family was forcibly taken to the Tuileries, a long-deserted Paris palace of the Bourbons. King Louis XVI was virtually a prisoner of the Commune.

From 1789 to 1791 the Assembly drafted the new constitution. The constitution created a state in which the king, as the executive, shared power with a legislature elected by citizens who paid at least a moderate amount of tax. Of gravest consequences were the Assembly's religious measures. Church properties were confiscated and nationalized in 1789 and religious orders suppressed in 1790. The clergy were required to take the oath on the Assembly's Civil Constitution of the Clergy. Few priests obeyed. When the Assembly declared that any priest refusing to obey would be banished from France, the king was roused to action and used his constitutional right of veto. This further incurred the wrath of the people, and the king was forced to support the measure.

In June, 1791, the king decided to flee to the border where loyal troops under General de Bouillé were waiting for him. It was thought that a coup from there might restore his authority. But the flight was brought to a disastrous halt at the little town of Varennes and the royal family was brought back in humiliation. On his return, the king agreed to accept the constitution.

Now "Liberty, Equality, Fraternity" became the motto of the people. The *sans-culottes*—revolutionaries of the poorest class—characteristically wore workingmen's clothing and red bonnets, symbols of the new order.

Meanwhile, the early sympathy shown in foreign countries for the revolution of "oppressed people" was wearing thin. Emigrés, mostly noblemen who had fled the country, were urging other nations to intervene. In France war was desired by royalists, who hoped it would lead to a restoration of absolute monarchy, and by republicans who wanted to spread the revolution abroad and also hoped that war would consolidate support for the new regime at home. Goaded by a veiled threat from the emperor of Austria and the king of Prussia regarding the security of the French king and a treaty signed by these two monarchs, France declared war on Austria on April 20, 1792. The French Revolutionary Wars had begun.

Early setbacks and rumors of treason by the king and queen excited the people to violent action. On June 20 an angry mob shouting threats and carrying signs saying "Down with the Veto" engaged in a riot ending in invasion of the Tuileries. This was followed on August 10 by a savage attack on the palace; the royal family fled to the Assembly for protection. The Commune, dominated by radical figures, became more influential and, under pressure, the Assembly suspended the powers of the king and ordered elections for a new body, the National Convention. The royal family was imprisoned in an old fortress, the Temple, on August 13, 1792. And the terrible, bloody "Reign of Terror" was on the way.

Thousands of aristocrats and royalist sympathizers—men, women and children—were arrested. The arrests were followed by the massacres of September second and third. Bloodthirsty mobs broke into jails and monasteries and butchered thousands of aristocrats, nobles and clergymen.

On September 21, 1792, the members of the Convention held their first meeting and abolished the monarchy, setting up the First Republic. In December, they tried the king for treason. He was found guilty and beheaded January 21, 1793. Queen Marie Antoinette was executed on October 16, 1793, and the king's sister, Princess Elisabeth, was guillotined on May 16, 1794. The two royal children, Marie Thérèse Charlotte, called Madame Royale, and her brother Louis Charles (after his father's death named King Louis XVII), were confined in the Temple until (it is presumed) the little king died of mistreatment and Madame Royale was exchanged for French political prisoners. On December 19, 1795, she was sent to relatives in Austria.

Although the foreign war ended on April 5, 1795,

with Prussia's "Peace of Bale," and the Reign of Terror had bled itself out with the guillotining of Robespierre and his cohorts on July 28, 1794, the Revolution continued to "eat its own children." Famines affecting the people persisted, as did riots and insurrections. The last of these insurrections, on October 5, 1795, was quelled by a new star on the horizon, Napoleon, thus ending the French Revolution.

LIFE AT VERSAILLES

I am the daughter of King Louis XVI and Queen Marie Antoinette of France. I am fifteen years of age, having been born on 19th December 1778.

I have decided to keep a journal, an account of our life and occurrences since that dreadful Monday, 13th August 1792, when my father, mother, brother, aunt, and I were imprisoned in this fortress called the Temple.

I was named Marie Thérèse Charlotte, but I am called Madame Royale, the title customarily given the first daughter of the king and queen of France. The name of my brother is Louis Charles. He is eight years old. When they killed my father he became King. That is the custom.

He is a rather naughty, spirited boy and he is always hungry. My mother used to say that he took after my father in that respect. In other respects he takes after my mother.

My father was rather stout and untidy and his sight

was poor. My mother said it was undoubtedly because he read so much and pored over charts and geography maps. He made them too. At one time he loved to tinker with locks, but my mother was happy when he stopped that as she said his hands were always dirty. Nevertheless, when a locksmith or a plasterer came to the palace to do some work, my father simply could not resist giving him a hand.

My father liked nothing so much as going early to bed and rising early in the morning to go hunting. He, too, kept a diary, and he was so mad about the hunt that when for some reason or another he could not go he wrote across the page for that day, "*Nothing.*" My mother used to tease him about this, for she said that that was what he wrote the day he had to stay to meet her and she hardly considered that complimentary.

My mother was very beautiful and lighthearted. She loved to dance. She was slender and graceful and she had hair like pale gold satin and sparkling blue eyes. Her lips were red as cherries but she did not like her mouth. Having come from Austria, she said that she had inherited the full Hapsburg lower lip.

My mother was almost fifteen when she married my father who was almost sixteen. His two brothers, the Comte d'Artois and the Comte de Provence, were thirteen and fourteen.

Before my mother came to France there was a proxy wedding ceremony in Vienna in which her brother Ferdinand stood in for the Dauphin of France and put the wedding ring on her finger for him. That was right and proper, for that was the custom. Of course, there would be another wedding ceremony after she reached the palace of Versailles. On the eve of the proxy wedding, a huge feast for fifteen hundred guests was held. The great ballroom was bright with thirty-five hundred candles and (though my mother had never met my father) so-called "torches of love" were everywhere, entwined with cherubs, garlands and flowers. Fireworks and Turkish music preceded the supper. My mother used to describe this with tears in her eyes.

My grandmother, the Empress Maria Theresa, had thought of everything, for hundreds of firemen stood ready with damp sponges to extinguish the sparks falling from the candles. She even had dentists on hand, should there be a sudden case of toothache.

My mother left for France two days later, 21st April 1770. There was a long procession of carriages, with cannons booming and bells pealing all along the way, and a continuous round of entertainment wherever she stopped. After crossing the Rhine, and following High Mass at the Cathedral of Strasburg, came a carnival with acrobats, dancing and singing in the streets—all to welcome the new Dauphiness to France.

It was a good thing that such excitement took up her mind for, although she was traveling with a very large entourage (her ladies, her tutor, the French ambassador, and the Prince of Starhemberg, special ambassador to the King of France charged with delivering the Dauphiness and the others), she had not been permitted to have any member of her family accompany her. Custom and distance considered, she knew that she would probably never see them again, so she cried herself to sleep every night.

On 16th May 1770 my father and mother were married with great ceremony in the chapel of Versailles: the Dauphin in gold cloth and diamonds, the Dauphiness in white, silver and diamonds. When they signed their names in the church register my mother was terribly embarrassed because she shook so that she made a big ink blot.

At first my mother did not have much to do except play with her dog, Mops, and study (she was trying to improve her French and she was taking music and singing lessons). She pined desperately for a friend in whom she might confide. Soon, however, she was caught up in a whirlwind of ceremony and merrymaking, which helped to make her forget her loneliness in a new land among strangers. She turned to pleasure to fill up the empty hours. In later years my mother said that she had been led astray by the acclamation and extravagances that seemed so natural to the French Court; that she and her group of young madcaps were pleasure mad; that her life was a continual round of balls, fireworks, parades, fun and games —the rule of youth but poor preparation for becoming the Queen of France. She said, "I was too young and thoughtless; now I know where I stand."

My august parents were only four years older than the day they were married when King Louis XV was stricken with smallpox and died. When they heard they were King and Queen they fell on their knees and cried, "Lord God, guide and protect us. We are too young to rule." But they soon got used to it.

Because of the importance of succession, my parents were anxious that a baby should be born and that it should be a boy. But when I was born and turned out to be a girl they loved me just the same. My mother told me, many times, that she said to me as soon as I was born, "Poor little one, you are not what we wished for, but you are not on that account less dear to me. A son would have been rather the property of the state. You shall be *mine*. You shall have my undivided care, and you shall share all my happiness and console me in all my troubles."

At my birth there was a salute of one-and-twenty guns and all the church bells rang. Wine, instead of water, flowed in the public fountains and the people were treated to bread and sausages. Alms were distributed to the poor and other good deeds were done.

When I was three years old my parents' fondest wish was realized—a son was born. He was named Louis Joseph Xavier. Then there was great rejoicing and the royal salute of one-hundred-and-one guns for the birth of a Dauphin was fired. That was right and proper, for one day he would be king.

All the guilds sent deputies to Versailles for nine days of celebration. They each brought a present for the King. Members of the chimney-sweeps' guild bore a chimney and perched on top were little chimney-sweeps singing sweetly; the sedan representatives presented a gilded chair with a little Dauphin in his nurse's arms; the cobblers carried baby shoes; the tailors, a tiny uniform of the Dauphin's regiment; and the blacksmiths, an anvil on which they struck musical chimes. Knowing my father's weakness for the locksmith's craft, what appeared from them but a large, complicated lock which required all my father's skill to open—then out sprang a tiny steel Dauphin!

Sadly, my brother the Dauphin was not strong and died before he was eight years old. But my brother Louis Charles had been born on 27th March 1785 and was, so my mother said, as strong as a little peasant. Another girl, Sophie Béatrix, was born later but died before she was a year old.

As I look now at the damp walls and iron bars of this cold gray prison, my former life seems like a fairy tale, almost impossible to believe.

We lived in the beautiful palace of Versailles, a short distance from the City of Paris. It had hundreds of rooms and housed thousands of attendants and courtiers. There were parks, gardens, and fountains. Nobles—ladies and gentlemen—dressed in velvets, feathers and jewels, ministered to their King and Queen. The King's musicians were in constant attendance; the Court played games and danced day and night.

My mother enjoyed this, and the balls, masquerades, and theatre, as well as the English sport of horse-racing, which my uncle, the Comte d'Artois, had introduced to Paris. But my father, the King, was much too busy hunting to be bothered with all that. My father said that my mother had gotten in with bad companions, but since they were mostly his brothers and other relatives, there was not much he could do about it. And, since he loved my mother very much, he said he wanted her to enjoy herself even if she was a little giddy.

Once my mother and aunt went out in the park with a party of friends and waited for the sun to rise. Some of the courtiers were scandalized but when my father heard about it he only laughed and said they would get a bad name. But they could not have, for the next day I heard people call out, "Long Live the King!" and then "Long Live Our Little Queen!"

My father did not like partying either. At night when my mother and her friends danced and gamed he went to bed. Eleven o'clock was as late as he would stay up, and once when my mother and some friends were going dancing they played a joke on him by putting the clock ahead. I believe my uncle, the Comte d'Artois, was the one who thought of it. He and my other uncle were not very nice to my father. They called him names like "spoil-sport" and showed him very little respect. I think it was because they would have liked to be King, but my father said he had no intention of obliging them. Later on, when my mother said they had lost no time in fleeing the country when they saw trouble coming, my father, who was a very charitable man, asked, What good would it have done for them to stay?

My aunt, Princess Elisabeth, was a great favorite with us all. Perhaps it was because she was so good and kind. She and my father were very religious, observing fast days without fail. They often read their prayer books. My father used to laugh and say that my mother was a good woman, but that she ought to read more. They both loved my brother and me so much, and they loved my aunt, too. My mother called her "Little Sister" (she had been only six years old when my mother came to France), and when we went to Saint-Cloud, Marly, Fontainebleau, or any of our palaces, she always went with us.

When we voyaged to Fontainebleau in the autumn, some of the Court had to be lodged in houses in town, as this chateau had only one hundred and seventy-two rooms.

At Marly on Sundays and holidays the fountains played and the people were admitted to the gardens where they could enjoy the fêtes. Here, after dinner and before the time for cards, it was the custom for the Queen and her ladies, in full Court dress, to be paraded around the park in little sedans with gold-fringed canopies, drawn by pages in the King's red and gold livery. Cards began at seven. It was the rule that the Queen and her ladies seat themselves at the gaming tables and the gentlemen request them to bet upon their cards with such gold or banknotes as they might present. My father disliked high play, and often showed his displeasure when a lot of money was won or lost. My mother thought it was fun.

Of all our palaces, the summer palace, the Petit Trianon, was the one my mother liked most. My father had given it to her for a New Year's present, and it was like a doll's house in size and furnishings compared to the other places. We loved to go there. We would loll on the grass without our hoops in simple cottons instead of the stiff brocades we wore at Court. We would play in the gardens, visit the chicken-runs or the cow-houses, and sometimes even help to make butter, for my mother had made this a farm. There were pigs and rabbits, and sheep with blue ribbons around their necks so we could lead them to pasture.

My mother had a little theatre built, too, and she and my uncles acted with the visiting actor troupe, while my father, the princesses and other members of Court were the audience. My father came to every performance, and was highly amused, though one time he did say, "It was royally ill-played." That was after my mother and my uncle had forgotten their lines. My brother, sitting on my father's lap, watched the prompter, too, groping for the words. In spite of the huge spectacles he wore, he could not seem to find them and, as everyone waited, my brother suddenly spoke out: "M. Campan, take off your big spectacles. Mama cannot hear you." My father thought that was very funny.

The Queen, my mother, used to breathe a sigh of relief when she could get away from the etiquette of Court life to relax and play at the Little Trianon. Some of the older ladies of the Court were shocked by this, especially

Mme de Noailles who had the post of Maid of Honor to the Queen. She was so steeped in ceremony that my mother, in private, had nicknamed her "Mme Etiquette."

Ceremony began with dressing my mother. It had to be done "according to Royal Etiquette." The Queen's Lady of Honor and Lady of Attire attended her along with the first Lady of the Chamber and two ordinary women. The Lady of Honor poured out the water for washing the Queen's hands and helped her put on her underwear; the Lady of Attire dressed her in her petticoat and helped her on with her gown. But, if a princess of the Royal Family entered, the Lady of Honor had to yield her privilege to her. Sometimes, in the cold weather, my mother would get chilly waiting for each garment to pass from hand to hand, and one day she even said right out loud, "How tiresome!"

Sometimes, though, my mother had breakfast in bed after her bath, and I would be allowed to go with her tire-lady, who brought her a pincushion and a book of swatches of her wardrobe. This was for the Queen to stick pins in the swatches of the gowns she wanted to wear that day: one for the dress, one for the afternoon undress, and one for the full evening dress for cards or supper parties. Often she let me choose and stick in the pins. Then she would kiss me and compliment me on my excellent taste. She would ask me which jewels she should wear: "Shall I wear the pearls or these diamonds?"

After this came M. Leonard, the Court hairdresser, for the dressing of my mother's hair. This was an important public ceremony with courtiers and ladies in attendance. It was great fun to see what effects he could manage with the hair of the Queen and her ladies. Sometimes he made the coiffures rise to three feet, and when the ladies went out they had to kneel in their sedans or carriages, or hold their heads out the window. He used feathers, flowers, ribbons—even toy houses and ships in full sail for ornaments. Each lady tried to outdo the other: one wore a rose that seemed to be growing out of her ear; at the touch of a hidden spring it opened from a bud and seemed to burst into full bloom. But my father said my mother put her in the shade by coming up with a whole blooming English garden—waterfall, silver-ribbon stream, and all!

Yet, with all of that, she did not forget to be charitable, and to teach her children to be thoughtful of the poor. One winter, when it was very cold and the poor people were suffering, my mother had toys brought from Paris. "I should have liked to give you these beautiful New Year's gifts, my children," she said, "but the winter is a very rigorous one. Many unfortunate people have neither bread to eat nor clothes to cover them. I have given all I can to relieve their misery, and now I have no money left for the purchase of presents. I ask you, therefore, to give up your toys this year." But she gave the toyman fifty louis for his expenses in coming to Versailles and to console him for having sold nothing.

She tried to cure her children of undue pride, also. From when I was about six, she saw to it that other children dined with me and that my guests were served first, saying, "You must do the honors." And when I was about nine she thought that I should learn to mix with the country children, so she gave a children's party every Sunday in the Trianon gardens. Lemonade and cakes were served and any child was welcome. My mother led off the dances to get things going; she was concerned because I did not like to join in. She thought I was "too serious." "Mousseline Serieux" was her pet name for me.

My mother loved children, no matter where they came from. She became the patron of many orphans and one time she was made the gift of a young black child from Senegal. She had the little boy baptized in the chapel of Versailles. Then, instead of allowing him to be put in service, she made it the duty of one of her pages to look after him in his growing up. When life became difficult for us, my mother took care to have this child safely settled in a home for children at Saint-Cloud. She made monthly payments for his care right up to the time we were taken to the Temple. She was terribly distressed later to hear that no one had the courage to assume responsibility for this poor black boy and that he had been cruelly turned out to die of hunger and cold.

My mother was fond of pretty clothes and jewels, but when she was thirty she gave up feathers and flowers in her hair and pink dresses; she said they were for the young.

THE QUEEN'S DIAMONDS

It was even before that—when I was born—that my mother gave up jewels. As befits royalty, the Dauphiness had come to France with some diamonds of her own and, upon her arrival, was presented with more jewels by King Louis XV.

Acquiring a taste for diamonds, she did buy some from the Court jeweler, Böehmer, before I was born, but she paid for them out of her own purse and in installments; it took her several years to catch up. My father presented her with a set of rubies and diamonds, but she went ahead and bought bracelets and chandelier earrings. She then found that she did not have enough money left to pay for them. She had to borrow from my father, who paid in four installments. He did not seem to mind; in fact it became a family joke that he said he was not surprised the Queen of France had no money in view of her taste for diamonds.

But, when I was born and he wished to give her a magnificent diamond necklace, she refused. She said that thereafter she would have no need, that her children would be her jewels. She told Böehmer that she found her jewel case rich enough, and that she would not be adding to it. She would have her jewels reset, if necessary.

In spite of this, he kept trying to sell her new pieces, especially that diamond necklace. When he could not persuade the Queen, he tried to make the sale by going to the King, knowing that my father loved to give my mother presents. But my mother said that it was too expensive, that she already had very beautiful diamonds, and that the money might better be spent on a ship for France.

To show how persistent Böehmer was, a year later he again offered the necklace to my father, proposing that it should be paid for in installments and in life annuities. My father suggested it to my mother, but again she refused. But she told him if he thought the bargain was really not bad, he might buy the necklace and keep it as a wedding gift for one of his children. My father said that that was looking too far ahead and that he would decline the offer.

Several months later, when I was with my mother one day, Böehmer appeared in the antechamber and requested an audience. My mother had no idea that it was to speak about the necklace twice-refused and kindly agreed to see him. Imagine her consternation, then, when he threw himself upon his knees, clasped his hands and burst into tears.

"Madame," he cried, "I am ruined and disgraced if you do not buy my necklace. I cannot outlive so many misfortunes. When I go hence I shall throw myself into the river."

"Rise, Böehmer," my mother said in disgust, "I do not like these rhapsodies; honest men have no occasion to fall on their knees to make their requests. If you were to destroy yourself, I should regret you as a madman in whom I have taken an interest, but I should not be in any way responsible for that misfortune. Not only have I never ordered the article which causes your present despair, but whenever you have talked to me about fine collections of jewels I have told you that I should not add four diamonds to those which I already possess. I told you myself that I declined to take the necklace; the King wished to give it to me but I refused him also; never mention it to me again. Divide it and try to sell it piecemeal, and let me hear no more about yourself. I am very angry with you for acting this scene of despair in my presence and before this child. Let me never see you behave this way again. Go."

My mother heard later that he had sold the necklace to a sultana in Constantinople. She said she was delighted to hear it, but that she could not understand how a sultan came to purchase his diamonds in Paris.

I am mentioning so much about diamonds because that necklace was to become a scandal and was to cause my mother great trouble. In 1786, when a government deficit was declared, the people accused their Queen of having "squandered the money of France on diamonds and wild extravagances." They refused to believe that my mother had not bought the necklace secretly after Cardinal de Rohan and a group of people, including Böehmer, said she had. My mother had them arrested, and Cardinal de Rohan was confined to the Bastille until his trial. He was acquitted, which was a terrible blow to my mother, for now the people vented all their rage on her.

This was all they needed, for it had been revealed by my father's finance minister that France was bankrupt; that, in fact, the government had been borrowing vast sums of money for twelve years. The people said this was mainly to pay for the extravagances of my mother, the Queen. Now, instead of calling her "Our Little Queen," they were calling her "Madame Deficit." They even hissed her, so she stopped going out in public. They shouted, Why, when *they* had done none of the spending, should France be bankrupt? They starved, they said, while France's Royal Family lived in sinful luxury and waste—why, the Royal Household alone cost France one sixth of its treasury! If that was so, it was also true that my mother was lacking in understanding of economic problems: "How could I have known," she cried in answer to the accusations, "when, if I asked for *fifty* thousand louis, they gave me a *hundred thousand*?"

My father brought in one finance minister after another to see what could be done, and my mother reduced our staff and simplified our way of living. Many of the Court, my mother's closest friends in some cases, left in indignation because they would no longer be receiving the royal favors and incomes to which they had long been accustomed through the graciousness of my parents.

The King, my father, called for an Assembly of Notables—the nobility and clergy—and asked them if they would share in the national burden of taxation, but they refused. Then he, together with Finance Minister Necker, did something that had not been done in one hundred and sixty years. He called for the States-General, which included the First Estate (the Clergy), the Second Estate (the Nobles) and the Third Estate (the Commons) to meet at Versailles so that all their grievances might be presented to the Crown.

On 5th May 1789 Versailles was swarming with people, for they had come from all over to see what was happening. We children watched the procession go by from the palace balcony, but this was just before my brother Louis Joseph died and he was not much interested. He suffered from rickets which had curved his spine so that my poor little brother was too weak to walk alone and had to be helped like a feeble old man. He brightened up, however, when the King's falconers came along with the hoods over their heads and those fierce-looking birds on their wrists.

My father had such hopes for this meeting. But there was so much discord from the Third Estate, the Commons, who were loudly demanding the people's rights, that it was thought best to end the meeting.

For the first time in history the Royal Decree to dissolve was defied. When the building was closed against them, the Third Estate moved to the indoor tennis court where they took an oath that they would not dissolve until the will of the people had been recognized. They vowed they would not separate until they had given France a constitution, and they called themselves the National Assembly, instead of the Third Estate.

My father wavered between what course of action he should take. His sympathies were always with his people, but my mother said that if he, the King, meekly acceded to their demands he would be undermining the heritage of his children. Necker was a friend of the people and disagreed with my mother. At last my father sided with my mother and banished Necker. The mood of the people was so ugly over this dismissal that my father decided to reinforce the Palace bodyguards and called up more troops. The people resented this and milled about in angry mobs. On 13th July they formed a parade, carrying a plaster bust of their friend Necker. They also carried a bust of the Duc d'Orléans, my father's cousin, a relative with whom we were not too friendly. Some said the people would like to make him King.

On the night of 14th July my father was awakened by his Grand Master of the Wardrobe, who always had the privilege of awakening him, and was told that a mob of thousands of Parisians had stormed the Bastille, had killed some people, and had released prisoners. My father was not alarmed. He just turned over and went back to sleep.

But the people continued to be rebellious, demanding that the King come to Paris. They even said that if he would not they would come and get him. My father reduced his troops and, on 17th July, with only a few bodyguards and a few nobles, bravely went to Paris to calm the people.

My mother was afraid for his safety, and after he left she shut herself up with us, her children, all day. She was so concerned that they would keep the King, my father, a prisoner in Paris she had traveling clothes laid out for all of us, and she sent orders to have a carriage and horses in readiness. She composed an address to the Assembly and practiced it aloud until she knew it by heart. It began: "Gentlemen, I come to place in your hands the wife and family of your sovereign; do not suffer those who have been united in Heaven to be put asunder on earth. . . ." Every time she came to this she would burst into tears and say, "They will not let him return."

My mother sent for several of her attendants but the doors were locked, their rooms empty. They had fled in terror. A death-like silence filled the palace. My little brother stood with his face pressed against the window-pane, looking anxiously up the Avenue de Paris, eagerly awaiting our father's return. "Why should they hurt Papa?" he asked, "he is so good."

You can imagine our joy when my father returned that night! My mother, my aunt, my brother and I threw ourselves into his arms. My mother was astonished to see him wearing the new tricolor cockade in his hat but he said that he had put it on to please the people, that he had forgotten all about it, and that it did not matter. All that mattered, he said, was that things had ended amicably. "Happily," he said, "no blood has been shed, and I swear that never shall a drop of French blood be shed by *my* order."

Les honneurs (traditional posts of honor) were abolished, but old and faithful friends like Mme de Tourzel and Mme Campan continued to serve us in posts that no longer existed. However, the regiment of French guards abandoned its colors, leaving only a single company of grenadiers faithful to their posts. We learnt that they had deserted to enroll in M. de La Fayette's new National Guard. My father then had the Flanders regiment brought to Versailles and a dinner was given to welcome them, at which the Royal Family appeared. They cheered us, and my mother wept.

THE MARCH ON VERSAILLES

On 6th October 1789, when I was almost twelve years old, something terrible happened.

Very early in the morning I was awakened by loud cries, the beating of drums and other great noises outside the palace. I hurried out of bed to the window. People were filling the parade ground and the courtyards; men and women armed with scythes, sticks and pikes were shaking them at the bodyguards. They were waving a blue standard with red flames on it, and they were shouting for bread.

Suddenly they rushed the guards; a few broke through and ran up the King's staircase. I could hear someone crying out, "Where is the Queen? We want the Queen! We are going to cut off her head, fry her liver, and that won't be the end of it!" Then I heard hard fighting.

At this point Mme de Tourzel, our governess, entered my room with my brother. We were all in nightclothes.

Mme de Tourzel was very calm and said, "Do not be frightened, my dears. We are in no danger." She explained to me that there was no bread in Paris, that some were starving to death, and that the people thought that flour was being hoarded at Versailles.

My brother was rubbing his eyes and, being only four years old, was too young and sleepy to know or care what was happening. I did not know whether he or Mme de Tourzel had heard what I had, so I said nothing. We sat down to wait, but my brother grew restless and said he wanted his breakfast.

After what seemed like a long time, M. de La Fayette, who was in charge of order, came to us with several grenadiers and escorted us to my father's private rooms.

My father was sitting in a chair, and my mother and aunt were standing at an open window. They all looked very disheveled. I ran to my father, and my brother climbed up on a chair in front of my mother.

"Mama, I'm so hungry," he said. My mother had tears in her eyes but she told him he must be patient and wait till the turmoil was over. She glanced out of the window then, and whatever she saw must have upset her, because she cried out, "They are going to kill my son!"

M. de La Fayette went to the window and looked out. Then he turned to my mother and said, "They are calling for you, Madame. I think it necessary that you show yourself in order to calm the people. They are calling for the Queen."

"Show herself!" cried my aunt. "After the butchery that has gone on here? After the Queen had to flee by the secret staircase to the King to save her life? After they forced their way into the Queen's bedroom and stabbed her bed with their pikes?"

M. de La Fayette insisted that my mother had to show herself in order to calm the people, so she said, "In that case, I shall do it, even if it costs me my life."

She started to walk over to the balcony and my brother and I ran to her side. She took each of us by the hand and stepped out on the balcony, but a man in the crowd called out, "No children!" so she handed us back to Mme de Tourzel.

M. de La Fayette then followed my mother out, and to show his allegiance to his Queen, bowed low and kissed her hand.

I later learnt that one of the conspirators aimed his firing-piece at her, but did not dare to complete his crime.

When M. de La Fayette led her back into the room, the crowds were cheering her, but they were still shouting "To Paris! . . . The King to Paris!"

My mother again had tears in her eyes, and she said, "They will compel us, the King and me, to go back with them to Paris, while they carry in front the heads of our bodyguards, on the tips of their pikes."

The people had gotten ugly again. Over and over they chanted, "The King in Paris! . . . We want the King in Paris!"

My father, who had been sitting as if in a dream, rose and went to the balcony, although my mother said she feared they would kill him.

"The French do not commit regicide," he said. "I am as much a Frenchman as a King."

He told the people that he was willing to go to Paris, but only on condition that he would be accompanied by the Queen and his family. And he asked that they spare the lives of his bodyguards, some of whom had already been killed or injured; we were not sure which.

M. de La Fayette then added his entreaty and made the people renew their oath of allegiance in the presence of their King. He even allowed some members of the bodyguard to go out on a balcony where they threw their shoulder-belts down to the crowd, handed their hats to the grenadiers and, borrowing forage caps, put them on their own heads.

The people cheered wildly then. But their cheers were not just for my father. They cried, "The Nation Forever!" and "Liberty Forever!" as well as "The King Forever!"

M. de La Fayette, on his side, never ceased to harangue the rioters, but his words had no effect, and the tumult continued. He told them that my father consented to return with them to Paris; he said he could assure them that my father had given him his word. This promise calmed them a little; and while the carriages were being made ready to start, all the family returned to their rooms to dress, for we still wore our nightcaps.

THE TUILERIES

The King, my father, with his family, left Versailles at noontime. Little did we know we would never see it again.

My mother had been right, for the heads of two guards, on pikes, led the entourage. They still had on their powdered wigs and hats. Mme de Tourzel shielded my brother's eyes from the bloody sight as we got into the carriage.

In spite of my father's plea, two more of the bodyguards suffered neck wounds. Each had to be held up by two officers with drawn swords in their hands. The other guards on foot were unarmed, though they were surrounded by men with sabres and pikes. Others of the bodyguard and National Guard were mounted on horses. I did not see how they could move, for men and women were pressing against them, forcing them to drink from what they held up, and ordering them to join in shouting, "Long Live the Nation!"

Men and women—I learnt that some men were dressed as women, and some women as nuns—wore the new red, white and blue cockades and carried tree branches. Some were astride the cannon in front and in back of our carriage, and after we started they never stopped firing their muskets. They were very drunk.

They ran alongside our carriage, too, shouting: "Bread, bread, we want bread!" And then they said, "We are bringing the baker, the baker's wife and the baker's boy!" I guess they did not insult me because I never could be King.

After riding like this for six hours (a trip that usually took two), we arrived at the town hall where the mayor, Bailly, was waiting. He greeted us with a speech, saying that it was a splendid day on which the Parisians at last were able to have the King and his family in their city. Then he derisively presented my father with the keys of the city on a gold plate.

My father answered, "I hope, sir, that my sojourn in Paris will bring peace, harmony and obedience to the laws. It is always with pleasure and confidence that I find myself among the inhabitants of Paris."

Some of the people could not hear him, so Bailly said, "His Majesty said that it is always with pleasure that he finds himself among the inhabitants of Paris."

My mother reminded him, in a loud voice, that the King had also expressed his *confidence.*

"You hear, gentlemen," Bailly sneered, "this is even better than if my memory had not betrayed me."

The King and Queen had to stand in the window, lighted by torches, so that everyone could see them. The people cheered, "The King Forever!" but again they shouted "The Nation Forever!" and "Liberty Forever!" We were then allowed to proceed to the Tuileries, a palace that had been deserted more than a hundred years before, when Versailles was built.

We reached there after ten o'clock. In the dim light of just a few candles it was a forbidding sight. Instead of our mirrored hall, glittering chandeliers, and comfortable furniture, we found broken windowpanes, doors that stuck opening and closing, and rooms completely dismantled. There were no beds.

"How ugly it is here, Mama," my brother said.

"My son," my mother told him, "Louis XIV managed to live here. It is not for us to make more difficulties than he did."

My father made no complaint. He was sleepy. "Let us all shake down as best we can," he said. "For myself, I am content."

My aunt said we could not have done better than to come to Paris, and that we should always be better off here than anywhere else.

But my mother could not be cheered. "What has happened during the last four-and-twenty hours seems incredible," she said. "No description of it could be exaggerated . . . and, indeed, whatever could be said would fall short of what we have seen and suffered."

And then she said a strange thing to my father: "Tribulation first makes one realize what one is."

The day after our arrival at the Tuileries there was a loud noise like gunfire in the gardens. My brother was terrified and ran to my mother, asking, "Is today yesterday again?" Then he looked at my father with a pensive air. When my father asked him what he was thinking about, my brother asked why the King's people, who formerly loved him so much, were all at once angry with him, and what had he done to make them punish him so.

My father took his son on his knee and said, "I wished, child, to render the people happier than they were; I wanted money to pay the expenses caused by wars. I asked my people for money, as my predecessors have always done; magistrates composing the *Parlement* opposed it; they said that the people alone had the right to consent to it. I assembled the principal inhabitants of every town, whether distinguished by birth, fortune, or talents, at Versailles; that is what is called the States-General. When they were assembled, they required allowances which I could not make, either with due respect for myself, or with justice to you who will be my successor. Wicked men inciting the people to rise have caused the excesses of the last few days; the people must not be blamed for them."

I do not know if my brother understood all this, but he seemed satisfied.

My mother, knowing how thoughtless and demanding my brother could be, made him comprehend that he must treat the commanders of battalions, officers of the National Guard, the newly-formed officials, and the Parisians about him with courtesy. When he was obliged to answer anyone, he would come and whisper in her ear, "Was that right?"

Before very long our new home was definitely improved. Furniture was brought from Versailles and repair men were put to work. And our staff, with the exception of a few who refused to come, were again with us.

My father's personal bodyguards were replaced by M. de La Fayette's National Guards, who were posted at the entrances; and M. de La Fayette himself insisted on paying my father a visit every night before he retired. My father did not much appreciate this; he said that it was a check to see that he was still there.

Our apartments looked out on the gardens—my mother and aunt were pleased at this—and consisted of my father's bedroom and reception rooms, a room for my aunt, one for my brother, and one for me. Also, there was a small drawing room.

My mother took the apartment closest to the gardens on the ground floor—a bedroom, reception room and dressing room.

The two floors were connected by two flights of steps, the Grand Staircase and a new staircase which led to our rooms upstairs. Only my mother and Mme de Tourzel had keys to the door opening on these stairs.

After my mother had breakfasted, she had her children brought down to her. She then attended Mass and returned to her room until dinner time. We all dined together, then my father and mother played a game of billiards. She thought this was good exercise for my father, for he no longer went hunting. He did a lot of reading and dozing; sometimes he got grumpy and didn't speak to anyone for days. After supper the whole family gathered together in the big drawing room.

My mother's best friend, Mme de Lamballe, was with us, as well as a few others. My uncles and their families had their own places. There were no parties or balls.

My father still went to bed at eleven, and my mother retired to her own rooms. She now did a lot of reading and writing.

We all felt sorry for my little brother who, being so young, could not understand the change. My mother called him "a cabbage of love" but she was determined not to spoil him.

Mme de Tourzel once let me read a letter my mother wrote her when she agreed to become his governess:

"Our affection for him must not lack an element of severity," she wrote, "we must not forget that we are bringing him up to be a king. He has absolutely no conception of the exalted position he occupies, and it is my strong desire that he should continue to be simple-minded in this respect, for our children learn all too soon into what rank they have been born.

"He is extremely fond of his sister. Whenever anything gives him pleasure—whether it be some excursion, or a present that has been given him—his first instinct is to ask that she shall have a like indulgence."

He is a sweet child.

PRISONERS IN THE TUILERIES

It was now June 1791 and my father and mother were growing impatient with the restricted life we were leading. They hardly ever went out, and things they heard made my mother say that, if we remained there, we would have no alternative but to accede to every demand or else perish under the sword which was perpetually suspended over our heads.

The fact that we were prisoners had been brought to bear on 18th April, when we entered a carriage for a drive to Saint-Cloud for some fresh air and were forcibly prevented from leaving the Tuileries. We were seated in the carriage and waiting for the horses to be hitched, when we realized that an angry crowd was preventing this from being done.

M. de La Fayette eventually appeared and, as commander of the National Guard, ordered that we be allowed to leave. No one paid any attention to him. He ordered the mayor to hoist a warning signal and was laughed at. He tried to address the crowd, who were shouting and hurling insults at our carriage, and he was shouted down.

We sat there for more than two hours; then my father asked that our carriage be wheeled back to the carriagehouse and said that we would return to the palace.

The National Guard agreed to protect us, and my mother raised her voice so that all could hear.

"Yes," she said, "we count on your devotion. Still, you must admit that we are no longer free."

Shortly after that happened, my father read an article by Marat in *The Voice of the People*, a newspaper which one of the servants (certainly a spy) had purposely left for us to see. My father read it aloud: "Are you imbeciles that you take no steps to prevent the flight of the royal family? Parisians, stupid that you are, I am weary of saying to you over and over again that you should lock up the Austrian woman, her brother-in-law, and the rest of the family. The loss of one day might be disastrous to the nation, might dig the graves of three millions of Frenchmen."

THE FLIGHT TO VARENNES

The night of 20th June 1791 I was awakened by my mother softly knocking at my door.

Earlier that day she had taken my brother and me for a walk and, while kissing me, she had whispered that we might be separated for a little while, but that I was not to worry about it. I did not understand this, and did worry until I dozed off to sleep.

It was after ten o'clock and I was frightened, as I did not know who was knocking. I called to Mme Brunier, who slept in my room, and she admitted my mother, who told her to dress me at once in a previously-selected simple cotton dress with little flowers on a gosling green ground.

In the meantime my mother had gone to wake my brother. She told him he must get up, that he was going on a long journey to a fortress where there would be plenty of soldiers, and where he would command his regiment. She said this because she knew he was mad about soldiers. Although very sleepy, the little boy murmured something about getting him his sword and boots.

Mme de Tourzel knew what was going on. A long time before, she had taken the precaution of having a little cloth dress and bonnet made, presumably for her daughter, but really for just this occasion. She now dressed my brother in this disguise, telling him that first we were going to a masquerade.

We reached the door where my mother was waiting, and she kissed Mme de Tourzel and said to her, "The King and I are entrusting to you, Madame, with complete confidence, that which we hold most dear in the world. Everything is ready. Now go."

I remembered then that my mother and father had seemed to me greatly agitated during the day, and much occupied, without my knowing the reason. After dinner they had sent my brother and me into another room and shut themselves in their own, alone with my aunt. I knew later that that was the moment when they told her of their plan for escaping from the way we were living.

My mother opened the outer door herself, looked carefully up and down, then beckoned. Mme de Tourzel, my brother and I hurried to the waiting coach where M. de Fersen, a Swedish nobleman in the service of France, was dressed as a coachman.

We drove along the quays to waste time, and returned by way of the Rue Saint-Honoré for the rest of the family. We had to wait three-quarters of an hour before they could slip away. M. de Fersen acted out his part. He whistled, gossiped with a real hackney-coachman who happened along, and took snuff from his snuffbox.

Mme de Tourzel seemed startled when I said, "There

is M. de La Fayette." She hid my brother under her skirts, telling us not to be alarmed. M. de La Fayette was with Bailly, but they both passed without paying any attention. Soon my aunt joined us, and stepped on my brother who was still under Mme de Tourzel's skirts. Little as he was, he had the courage not to cry out. But it was not till after twelve o'clock that my father came. He said that he had been detained by M. de La Fayette's nightly chat, and that he could not show any eagerness to end it. Then he had to go to bed to fool his valet, get up and put on his disguise of plain dark clothes, a rough wig and a lackey's hat.

My mother could not leave until after my father did, and my father was very concerned. When at last she came, he hugged and kissed her, and said, "Oh, how glad I am that you've come." Then everybody kissed every one else.

My mother was wearing plain dark clothes, too, and a thick veil covered her face. Mme de Tourzel was to be the "lady" and was to be called Mme de Korff. My mother was to be called Mme Rochet, and she was to be the governess of Mme de Korff's *two* girls. My father was to be known as Durand, the steward, and my aunt, the lady's maid. They all joked about the masquerade.

But we ran into trouble at once.

M. de Fersen, fearing that the three loyal members of the bodyguards who were to meet us had taken a different route from the one planned, decided to take the longer way to meet up with them rather than drive through the gates of Paris, a danger spot. That put us back a half hour, and then we ran into a wedding celebration with bright lights and crowds of people. Luckily, they paid no attention to us. But between Nintré and Châlons the horses broke their harness straps and it took an hour to make repairs.

During this time my father got out of the carriage

and went into an empty stable. My brother and I did not get out then, but we did later when the postilions dismounted as the carriage climbed steep grades. It was thought that the air and exercise would do us good.

We left our horses near the gate of Clichy where we found a coach waiting. M. de Fersen drove us as far as Claye, where we were to take the post-coach. When M. de Fersen left us, my father expressed his gratitude and the hope of meeting him again soon.

Now we were installed in a large coach which had been fitted out with every comfort. My father began to talk about his plans for the future. First he would go to Montmédy to emphasize the decision he had taken, which was right and proper. He had no intention of leaving the kingdom, except when it was necessary to pass through frontier towns in order to reach the French town where he was to reside. He did not wish to leave his beloved France and his people, but he hoped to escape from intolerable conditions as far as the frontier towns, which were guarded and where he would find loyal troops. The Marquis de Bouillé was the general there and he had made plans to help his King. My father even entertained the thought that he might then head a march on Paris. But even if he had to stay, he would at least have protection until things quieted down.

My father was in very good spirits now and said, "Well, here I am, at last out of Paris where I have been drenched with so much bitterness. You can be sure that once in the saddle again, I shall be quite different from the man you have seen up to now."

I think he said this to assure my mother, who was always telling him to make up his mind.

He then read us the memorandum he had left to be

read to the Assembly. He had great hopes for the happiness he could restore, for the return of his refugee brothers and faithful retainers, and for the possibility of bringing back the Faith and removing the sanctions he had been forced to make upon the Church.

Then he laughed and said, "La Fayette must be feeling very much embarrassed now."

It was now morning. My father looked at his watch and remarked, "It is eight o'clock. When we have passed Châlons we shall have nothing to fear. We shall find the first detachment of our troops at Pont-de-Sommevel, and then we shall be out of danger."

But when we arrived at Pont-de-Sommevel we learnt that our couriers had found no trace of soldiers, and they had not risked asking questions for fear of arousing suspicion.

Going on, we found no soldiers at Orbeval, nor at Sainte-Menehould, but an officer did ride by our coach and say, quickly, "The arrangements have been bungled; I must be off, so as not to attract suspicion." Another horseman, a few minutes later, reined in his horse, peered in at us, then galloped ahead. We thought then that we might have been recognized.

Growing more fearful by the minute, we pressed on to Claremont where we were met by a colonel of the Dauphin's Regiment of Dragoons who had not left his post in spite of warnings. He told us that the country was in an uproar over the flight of the Royal Family, but that he intended to do his best to turn out his regiment and escort the King's carriage. However, he was afraid he could not count on this, and a refusal from his men might result in the King's arrest.

All he managed to do was to send an officer at full speed to dispatch a warning forward. But the officer, who did not know the way, mistook the road to Varennes and was too late. As we approached this town, we saw a man hiding in the bushes.

We believed we had been betrayed then, and we knew we were in a dreadful position.

7

DISCOVERY AT VARENNES

On reaching Varennes, just a few tens of kilometers away from Metz, our destination, we were unable to find any change of horses, which was now necessary, and there was nobody to tell us anything. One of the postilions even knocked on a door and inquired if anyone there knew anything about a fresh supply of horses which should have been waiting. They could give us no information.

Then my father offered the postilions money if they would attempt to drive on to the next post. They refused, saying the horses were too tired. So my father told them to drive us to the last inn in the town, and we would rest while the horses were resting.

It was now half-past eleven at night. An entire day had passed since we left Paris. We learned that every carriage was being stopped in front of the house of the mayor of the town, a man called Sauce, and occupants were obliged to show passports. We had gone too far to turn back. There was nothing to do but go on.

An officer in the growing crowd slipped up to our coach and whispered that there was a stream we could ford, and offered to get us across it. But my father, seeing the increasing excitement of the crowd, refused to subject us or the officer to possible fire.

By now the tocsin had been sounded, and the crowd, drawn by the church bell's warning, was growing more suspicious. They swarmed around our coach when we were stopped, and Mme de Tourzel haughtily said she was the Baroness de Korff from Frankfort, and she was in a hurry to get back. She refused to show papers.

At first my father declined to say who he was, or to leave the coach. But, after some more questioning and the promise that we would be permitted to leave after our signatures had been examined, he refused no more. He knew that we had been recognized.

We went into Sauce's house. My father said simply: "Here is my wife, here are my children; we adjure you to show us the consideration which Frenchmen have always shown to their King." We were told that we were under the protection of the law, and that we had nothing to fear.

By now a small company of our hussars had arrived and were assembling in front of the house, with swords drawn to protect us, facing men and women armed with pikes, rakes and scythes. Some men were shouting at the women to go back to their houses; some were shouting to take up stones to throw at the hussars if they started any trouble and tried to defend the King. Two pieces of artillery were placed by the townspeople at the ends of the street with the hussars in between. Later we learned that the guns were not loaded.

The front of Sauce's house was a sort of shop smelling of sausage and spices. My father asked for something to eat and was given bread and cheese and a bottle of wine.

My brother and I were taken to the upper floor and put in a big feather bed together. We immediately fell asleep, for we were very tired.

When we awakened the next morning, two National Guard deputies had arrived for M. de La Fayette had issued an order for the King's arrest. They were standing in the room where we were still in bed, and my father was reading the National Assembly's decree, suspending the King's powers and commanding him to return to Paris.

My father, after reading it, threw the paper on our bed saying, "There is no longer a King in France!"

My mother flew across the room, snatched up the paper and, crumbling it, threw it on the floor. She said, "I will not have my children soiled by contact with this document!"

One of the deputies picked up the paper indignantly, and my father made haste to distract his attention. Would they, he asked, allow two or three hours' more rest, as they could see for themselves how tired the children were?

The deputies conferred, but one of them said they must see about this. On leaving, they seemed to be in an agreeable frame of mind. However, when they reached the street they mixed with the crowd who were waving their scythes and sticks, and were now calling my father bad names. The people said, "We will get him, no matter what they do." Even the hussars, partly from fright and partly from thinking it was no use to try to defend the King, had joined the people.

One of the deputies told the crowd that my father did not want to start yet, but that this was just a ruse—delaying tactics used in the hope that he might be saved. This, of course, was true, for my father was still hoping that the loyal troops we had been expecting would find us.

Shouting "To Paris! To Paris!" some of the rowdy men turned our coach around and horses were put to. We could hear all this going on, and M. Sauce, as mayor, urged my father to go at once, or he could not guarantee his safety.

When we went out to our coach I could see my poor father listening for the sound of galloping horses. But the horses never came.

When we were about a league and a half from Épernay we were met by three deputies from the Assembly, Pétion, Barnave and Latour-Maubourg, who were supposed to take us in charge. We were astonished when Pétion opened the door and told my father that he and Barnave would ride with us. However, after they were in the coach and saw how crowded this made us, Pétion had the grace to say it would discomfort us too much.

My father said, with great civility, "I do not want any of those who have accompanied me so far to leave the coach. I beg you to sit down. We shall sit close and make room for you." He told us later that he was afraid they might try to separate us, and this he could not have endured.

My father, my mother and my brother were on the back seat, and my Aunt Elisabeth, Mme de Tourzel and I on the front. My mother took my brother on her lap, and looked amazed when Barnave placed himself between her and my father. Mme de Tourzel quickly took me on her lap, and Pétion sat between my aunt and us.

My aunt was worried about the people who had been loyal enough to come with us. She said, "I beg of you, do not allow a disaster to befall, do not victimize those who have accompanied us; spare their lives! The King had no intention of leaving France."

My mother had tears in her eyes, and both she and my aunt put their hands imploringly on the arms of the deputies.

My father said he hoped no harm would come to the three bodyguards who were sitting on the box and told of one nobleman who had had his throat cut within our sight. My mother asked, How could his own countrymen murder him, especially since he was one who had done so much good in his district?

To distract my brother, my mother danced him on her knee and I tried to play with him. Mme de Tourzel seemed angry and spoke only once. She turned and said, "As far as I am concerned, I have done my duty in remaining with the children who have been entrusted to me. They can do what they like with me; I have no cause to reproach myself. If I had it to do over again, I should do just what I have done."

Conversation dwindled after that.

We entered Dormans after midnight and found that they could accommodate us at an inn. They took us—the King and his family—to the upper floor where we had supper. Sentinels were posted at the door to every room.

My poor father was to sleep alone in a room, but there was only a rickety iron bed so he sat up all night in an armchair. It was difficult to sleep because the townspeople had collected to drink, sing, and dance around the inn. All night long we heard cries of "Long live the Nation!" and "Long live the National Assembly!"—even "Long live Barnave" and "Long live Pétion." No longer did we hear cries of "Long live the King!"

RETURN TO PARIS

We took our seats in the coach next morning between five and six, only this time Pétion sat between my father and mother, and Barnave between us.

We were uncomfortably close in the heat, and now my brother, being well rested, could not keep still. He teased me and ruffled my hair. He sat on Pétion's knee and chattered.

My father studied the regional maps he had with him, saying that we were now in such an area, district or locale. My mother said his interest in geography stood him in good stead.

My mother talked with Pétion about the education of her children. She said that no flattery should be allowed and that we always should be told the truth.

We were being roasted by the sun and choked by the dust, but could not close the windows, as the National Guard who had met us and the country people who lined the roads wanted to look in to see the King and his family.

However, when my mother started to eat a pigeon leg she pulled down the blind. The onlookers protested, and my aunt thought we should release the blind.

"No," my mother said, "one must have character; one must have character at all costs."

After she finished she drew up the blind and threw the bones out the window.

The mayor of la Ferté-sous-Jouarre had sent a messenger to invite the King to stop at his home, which was a pretty house with gardens and terraces overlooking the River Marne. My father invited the deputies to dine with him but they refused. They looked embarrassed, and said they had correspondence to attend to. So we had a fine dinner in private.

As we left there was a commotion, and people tried to break the ranks of the National Guards around our coach. A man fought his way through the crowd and got to the coach, swearing and making insulting remarks. Pétion stuck his head out of the window and the man said to him, "Here's a lot of fuss for a brute like that! Are they all in there? Take care, they are still talking of rescuing them. You are sitting with some very conceited people in there."

My mother said, "What a rude man!" My brother was frightened and whimpered, but Pétion said that the man was just cross with the Guards who had been rough with him.

By now everybody talked about everything. The deputies discussed freely what had set the people against us. For instance, Pétion referred to the newspaper my father read. My father answered, "I assure you that *I* don't read *The Friend of the King* any more than Marat does."

On reaching Meaux, the King, his family and the

deputies were offered the hospitality of the Bishop's palace. Sentries were at all the gates. As my father had no fresh underlinen, he borrowed a nightshirt.

When we resumed our journey the next morning at six, Barnave sat between my father and mother. We rode for twelve hours and my brother needed attention two or three times. My father unbuttoned his son's breeches and held the silver chamber-pot for him to relieve himself. The deputies seemed surprised that the King would do this.

Just before getting to Pantin there was a disturbance. National footguards joined the grenadiers, and the chasseurs, together with the grenadiers, tried to force the cavalry back. Men with bayonets ran around the coach, and we could hear them swearing through the open window. They said bad things about my mother and called her ugly names. Tears rolled down her cheeks, and she held my brother closely. He was crying in terror.

The two deputies, seeing this, called out the window sharply. A grenadier answered not to be afraid. No harm would be done to anyone; they would answer for that. But the honor of escorting the Royal Family belonged to them.

Apparently this was what was causing the trouble, and when the grenadiers were told they would have that post the uproar quieted down.

It appeared that all Paris had gathered in the Champs Elysées to see our humiliating return. The streets, roofs, gates, and even the trees were filled with people. And there was silence everywhere.

We crossed the river by the swivel-bridge which was immediately closed behind us. When we came to the iron gateway leading into the palace, the guards closed in on our bodyguards on the seat with fixed bayonets and terrible curses. But Pétion ordered them, in the name of the law, to restrain themselves. The terrified men were ordered down and were treated somewhat roughly, but not really harmed, perhaps because M. de La Fayette came up on horseback and, in the midst of the bayonets, spoke sternly.

My father got out; there was silence. My mother followed, and was greeted with voices screaming hatred and violent expressions of disapproval. But when my brother and I alighted we received smiles and endearments. The crowd followed us up the staircase, pressing against us. My father and mother had my brother between them. One of the deputies took me in his arms to carry me through. In vain did I cry for my aunt; the noise was now so loud that she could not hear me.

When we reached the royal apartments my father and mother leaned against the furniture, looking very tired. A group of deputies arrived, and we could not believe our ears. One of them approached my father and said to him, as if his King were a little boy who had been mischievous, "That was a nice way to behave! That comes of having bad advisers. You are a good man, and you are liked, but see what a mess you have gotten into!" Then the man burst into tears.

The deputies ordered M. de La Fayette to place Mme de Tourzel under supervision and gave him custody of the King. He said he could not be responsible if he could not have sentinels placed even in the King's bedroom, but that he would have to have a ruling from the Assembly. Then they left.

THE ROYAL FAMILY UNDER GUARD

Residence in the Tuileries seemed to be much as before, except that we were kept under closer watch. The National Guard did not allow my mother to lock her doors at night, so she could not sleep very well. A guard sat in the space between the two doors of the drawing room and the bedroom so that he could keep an eye on her at all times.

The door of the drawing room remained open all day, too, but my father kept closing it. An officer of the guard flung it open once, and said severely: "I beg that this door not be shut; such are my orders!"

Since my mother could not sleep being watched, she was granted the favor of having a curtained bedstead placed before her bed for her first-woman to lie upon. This prevented the guard from having his eyes directly on his Queen. This pleased my mother, for she said sleep gave respite in sorrow, and that one was free at least while one slept.

One morning we were warned that there would be

another riot, that a mob was marching on the Tuileries. My mother's waiting woman asked that the Queen not be awakened, as she had not fallen asleep until dawn.

My father agreed. He said, "It is good to see her take a little rest. Her sufferings increase my own."

When my mother awoke, the danger had passed, but on hearing of the alarm her eyes filled with tears. "Elisabeth was with the King and I was sleeping," she wept. "I, who wish to die at his side! I am his wife. I do not wish him to incur any dangers without me."

Tempers became very short after that, and my mother and my aunt, instead of affectionately calling each other "sister" often quarreled. My father hardly spoke at all.

My uncles, with their families, had successfully fled the country, but my father had promised the Assembly that he would stay in Paris and, because he was an honorable man, he made no more attempts to escape his fate.

My mother accused my aunt of being sympathetic toward her two brothers across the frontier who, according to reports, were being indiscreet in words and actions that could be harmful to us. The Comte de Provence, it seems, had declared himself Regent and had set up a Ministry at Coblentz.

"Cain! Cain!" my mother cried on hearing this.

My aunt replied that my mother did not trust any one; my mother said, How could she?

By September, 1791, the Constitution was completed and on the fourteenth my father went to the National Assembly to swear loyalty to the newly formed constitution. They expressed satisfaction at their King's acceptance and, a few days later, declared a constitutional monarchy, which they said they had "decided to permit."

My aunt said, "They will be busy in taking from the King the right to wear his crown, which is about all that is left to him."

My mother grew very angry. "What can we expect . . ." she said. "Nothing but fresh outrages. As for myself, I could do anything, and would appear on horseback, if necessary. But if I were really to begin to act, that would be furnishing arms to the King's enemies; the cry against the Austrian, and against the sway of a woman, would become general in France; and moreover, by showing myself, I should render the King a mere nothing. A Queen who is not Regent ought, under these circumstances, to remain passive and prepare to die."

Because of the decree by the National Assembly depriving the King of custody of the Crown jewels, my mother had already given up those generally worn for State occasions. She had preferred, and still had, the twelve brilliants called the *Mazarins* (named after the Cardinal who had made a gift of them to the treasury), a few rose-cut diamonds and, of course, the *Sanci.* These, she decided, should be placed with the Crown jewels. She made up her mind that she would deliver them with her own hands to the commissioner named by the Assembly. She offered him also a rope of pearls of great beauty. She told him that this had been brought to France by Anne of Austria and that, since it had been designated by that Princess specifically for the use of the Dauphinesses of France, King Louis had placed it in her hands on her arrival in this country. But she now considered it national property.

"That is an open question, Madame," answered the man.

"Sir, it is one for me to decide," my mother said, "and it is now settled."

On 7th February 1792, Emperor Leopold of Austria and the King of Prussia signed a treaty confirming their meeting at Pilnitz the summer before, at which they had expressed their concern about the King of France. They called upon other governments to join with them in correcting the situation. They stated that they themselves were prepared to cooperate "with interfering by effectual measures." This threw the French people into a raging frenzy. On 20th April 1792, after violent debates in the National Assembly, France declared war on my mother's native Austria.

Now they tried to provoke my father in every way. One of the schemes was to make the King, a devout Catholic, avow that priests who refused to swear loyalty to the new Constitution were to be exiled from France. My father made use of his constitutional right of the veto and refused to consent.

My mother's hair was turning white. Whenever a church bell sounded she thought it might be the beginning of the tocsin for an assault on the Tuileries.

We had not long to wait.

A RIOT

On 20th June 1792 there was a demonstration in front of the hall of the National Assembly.

A few days before, my father had refused to sanction the order for the deportation of priests and had used his constitutional right to veto, which was right and proper. We learnt that the people were frantic, and cried out, "If the King gets this veto, what is the use of the National Assembly? We are slaves—all is done!"

Now they were marching up and down, carrying signs saying, "Down with the Veto!" "Warning to Louis XVI!" and "Liberty or Death!"

My mother, when she heard this, gave vent to her feelings. She said, "These people will have no sovereigns. We shall fall before their treacherous, though well-planned tactics; they are demolishing the monarchy, stone by stone."

My poor father, torn between one thing and another,

said, "Among ourselves we can speak frankly. I know I am scourged with weakness and irresolution, but no one has ever been in my position. I missed it three years ago. That was the time to go. Since then I have never caught up. I have been deserted by everyone."

At that moment, the crowds that had been demonstrating in front of the Assembly were heard outside crying that they had cannons and they would break our doors down if we refused to open them. They swept past the guards and into the palace.

My father and aunt were hemmed in one room and my mother, brother and I, together with Mme de Lamballe and Mme de Tourzel, in another.

When they found my father, this ruffian mob demanded that he withdraw his veto. When he refused, they spat vile threats. A terrible man by the name of Rocher said, "Ha! I am going to treat myself to a glass of your blood." Others also threatened to kill him. My father, unafraid, talked to them quietly.

Meanwhile, my mother's bodyguards, uneasy on her behalf, hurried us into the empty council chamber. As we huddled against the wall, they pushed a heavy table in front of us, and then stationed themselves in three rows in front of it.

When the furious mob broke into this room, they ordered the guards to step aside so they could get a good look at us. The guards stood their ground.

My mother, who had been in tears, now grew angry. She drew my brother, who was standing on the table in front of her, into her arms. A furious woman rushed forward and shrieked into my mother's face, "It is you who have caused the misery of the nation, you—you Austrian woman!" My mother answered calmly, "If you have been told so, you are deceived. As the wife of the King of France, and mother of the Dauphin, I am a Frenchwoman. I shall never see my own country again—I can be happy or unhappy only in France. I was happy when you once loved me."

A man called Santerre said to her, "You have been misled. The people wish you no harm. If you liked, there would not be one of them who did not love you as sincerely as you love that little boy. Besides, you need not be afraid, for no one will do you harm."

My mother answered: "I have not been misled, I have not been deceived, and I am not afraid. There is no occasion for fear; why should anyone be afraid who is among decent folk?"

One of the rogues took off his revolutionary red bonnet and offered it to my brother, who was frightened. At this, my mother said to the officers, "This is too much, and passes the limit of endurance!" But a half-naked woman ran forward and forced the bonnet on the poor little boy's head, while others made us put their tricolor cockades on our heads.

I do not know what would have happened if Pétion and my aunt had not then arrived on the scene. My aunt whispered to my mother, "The King is safe," and they fell into each other's arms, all past displeasure forgotten.

Pétion dispersed the crowd, telling them to go home "in the same orderly way" they had come. My mother, who had been so brave, burst into tears. She wept bitterly.

We learned that when Pétion had finally arrived he told my father he had just heard of the situation.

"That is surprising," my father said, "for this has

been going on for two hours!" When Pétion started to protest, my father said, "Be silent, sir; I know your thoughts."

We learnt, too, that my father had acceded to their wishes to put on the red cap to quiet them.

On the twenty-fourth of July there was a Prussian Declaration of War in the name of both the Emperor of Austria and the King of Prussia that threatened France with military measures if French royalty were meddled with further.

TO THE ASSEMBLY FOR PROTECTION

At midnight on the ninth of August, Attorney General Roederer and others came to my father and warned him that there would be another march on the Tuileries. He urged my father to take his family to the National Assembly hall that adjoined the Tuileries and had been, in fact, the indoor riding school of the palace. There we would be under the protection of the deputies. My father left the room without answering.

My mother sent a message for Mme de Tourzel to awaken my brother and me and bring us to her. We came, along with kind Mme de Lamballe who had been safely out of the country but who had returned from England to be with my mother in her bad moments.

It was so hot that the leaves had fallen off the trees, and my mother had not been able to sleep.

Now she said, "This is a conflict of forces. We have come to the point where we must know which is going to prevail—the King and the Constitution, or the rebels."

At this point there was shouting and booing in the garden and drummers were beating the call to arms. M. Roederer put his head out of the window. He said, "My God, it is the King they are booing! What the devil is he doing down there? Come quickly, let us go to him!" He and his men ran down the stairs.

My father was brought back, out of breath and red in the face. It seems he had gone down to rally his guards, but when he got there he did not know what to say, so he only made matters worse. Some artillery men had even dared to turn their cannon against their King!

My poor father. I remembered then what I had heard my mother say once to Mme Campan, her first lady of the bedchamber: "The King is not a coward; he possesses an abundance of passive courage, but he is overwhelmed by an awkward shyness, a mistrust of himself, which proceeds from his education as much as from his disposition. He is afraid to command, and above all things, dreads speaking to assembled members. He lived like a child, and was always ill at ease under the eyes of Louis XV until the age of twenty. This constraint confirmed his timidity."

After M. Roederer returned with my father he pleaded, "Sire, your Majesty has not five minutes to lose."

My mother said that we had a strong force in the palace but he answered, "Madame, all Paris is on the march." Then he turned to my father, who was sitting staring at the floor, and asked permission to escort us to the Assembly.

My father raised his head and looked at M. Roederer. Then he turned to my mother and said, "Let us be going."

As he rose to his feet, my aunt came from behind his chair and said, "M. Roederer, will you answer for the life of the King?"

He said yes, that he would walk in front, but that there should be no one from the Court, and there should be no other escort than the members of the department who would surround the Royal Family, and the men of the National Guard who would march in line on both flanks as far as the National Assembly.

"Very well," my father said. "Will you give the orders?"

My mother said, "What about Mme de Tourzel, my son's governess? And Madame de Lamballe?"

Yes, he said. They could come, too.

When we reached the bottom of the great staircase my father stopped and said, "What is going to happen to all the people remaining up there?" No one answered.

Mme Campan had remained in my mother's apartments. We learnt later that some men with drawn sabres rushed up the stairs, seized her and thrust her to their feet. But some of the Queen's other waiting women threw themselves at the ruffians' feet and held their blades away from her. Just then someone called from the bottom of the staircase, "What are you doing up there? We don't kill women." Her assailant quitted his hold on her and said, "Get up, you jade; the nation pardons you."

When we were under the trees we sank up to our knees in the piled up leaves. "What a lot of leaves," my father remarked, "they have begun to fall very early this year."

My brother, holding my mother's hand, was amusing himself by kicking the leaves against the legs of the persons walking in front of him. My aunt was holding tight to my hand and Mme de Tourzel and her daughter were supporting Mme de Lamballe who was trembling so she could hardly walk.

When we reached the hall, my father made an address. He said: "I have come here to prevent a great crime from being committed, and I am convinced that I could not be in a safer place than in your midst, gentlemen."

The president of the Assembly replied that the King could depend on the firmness of the National Assembly, but that they were sworn to defend with their lives the rights of the people and the constitutional authorities. They also said that it was against the rules for them to proceed with their debates with us there.

They then took us to the minute-writer's office. This room was so low the grown-up people could not even stand up straight. It had two or three stools and a bench, and an iron grating separated it from the hall. Not a breath of air could enter, and we were compelled to spend eighteen hours in this steaming cubbyhole.

All at once the boom of the gunnery was heard and men were saying it was coming from the Tuileries. Then someone shouted, "Here come the Swiss Guards!" Soon we heard the rattle of gunfire. There were shouts and cries coming from outside and inside now, saying that the King's Swiss Guards had fired on the people—had lured the citizens and then shot them down. There were curses and shouts demanding the death of the King.

My father sent an order for the Swiss Guards to cease firing, but before morning more than a thousand lives had been lost.

All at once, to our horror, we saw some of the faithful guards and nobles being chased into the Assembly hall by rogues who struck them down without mercy. They brought in my father's own servants who, with the utmost impudence, gave false testimony against him, while others boasted of vile things they had done. These were followed by looters who triumphantly strewed silverware, cash-boxes, letters, even our toys, and anything else they could pick up over the desk of the president of the Assembly.

We listened as men mounted the tribune to lie about and denounce my mother and father. They cried, "Death to the Austrian woman!" "Death to the King!" and "Death to the Aristocrats!" We heard my father, the King, deposed and his veto abolished.

At last some one brought us food and water. My mother took a glass of water; my father ate; my brother and I fell asleep. My mother did not break her fast until we were taken to the Convent of the Feuillants, which had been confiscated and where bedrooms were made up for us. Next day we were taken back and heard the King and Queen branded as oppressors of the people. We heard them discuss what should be done with the King and where he should be kept.

For three long days we listened until it was declared that the King was suspended from his functions and a new municipal government, the Commune, was formed.

It was decreed that the Temple was the only place to ensure our safety. We were to be conducted there "with all the respect due to misfortune." The attorney for the new Commune, M. Manuel, was to accompany us. The Temple—so-called because in olden days it had been the fortress of the Knights Templar—was as sinister-looking as the Bastille. It consisted of a small castle with a round tower at each corner, narrow windows, and an inner court which, we would find, the sun hardly ever reached. We were to live in this fortress.

Towards three in the afternoon, Manuel, accompanied by Pétion, came to take the Royal Family away. They made us all get in a carriage with eight seats. Then they crowded in with their hats on their heads, shouting "Long Live the Nation!" They had the driver go slowly, as throngs pressed themselves against the carriage, shrieking, spitting, and hurling insults. They had the cruelty, too, to point out to my parents things that would distress them—for instance, the statues of the kings of France thrown down from their pedestals, even that of Henri IV, before which they stopped and compelled us to look.

We learnt that the guillotine, the official instrument to cut off people's heads, had been set up in the Place du Carrousel.

IMPRISONMENT IN THE TEMPLE

The King, my father, arrived at the Temple with his family on Monday, 13th August 1792, at seven in the evening.

The gunners wished to take my father to the tower and leave us in the castle. But Manuel had received orders from the Commune, while on the way, to take us all to the tower. The gunners were angry about this, but Pétion calmed them down and we went into the castle. The men from the municipality kept an eye on my father. Pétion went away but Manuel stayed.

My father had supper with us. My brother was dying to go to sleep. At eleven o'clock Mme de Tourzel took him to the tower, which was definitely going to be our residence. My father and the rest of us went up to the tower at one in the morning. Nothing had been prepared for us. My aunt slept in a kitchen and it seems that Manuel was ashamed when he took her there.

On the next day, my father came to have breakfast

with my mother and afterwards we went to look at the great halls, where they said they would make some more rooms because the little tower, where we were, was too small for so many people.

After dinner, when Manuel and Santerre had come, we went and walked in the garden. They had complained very much about the women servants who had accompanied us, and when we arrived we found others chosen by Pétion to serve us. We did not want them.

Soon afterwards, they brought a paper from the Commune ordering the persons who had come with us to leave. My father and mother objected, and so did the municipality people who were on guard at the Temple. The order was revoked for the time being.

All of us spent the day together. My father did geography with my brother, and then my mother did history with him and made him learn some poetry by heart. My aunt gave him an arithmetic lesson.

My father was happy to find a collection of books, which occupied his time. My mother had her embroidery. The municipal guards were very familiar and showed little respect for my father. There was always one of them who kept him in sight.

At one in the morning on the night of the 19th-20th August, they brought an order from the Commune, saying that all persons not belonging to the Royal Family were to be taken away from the Temple. Cléry, my father's valet, was allowed to stay.

My mother took my brother into the room with my aunt. We were only separated from my mother by a little room which was occupied by a municipal guard and a sentry.

My father remained in his room upstairs and, knowing that they were preparing other quarters for him, he did not mind. As there were fewer people, he no longer felt crowded, and besides, he was nearer to my mother. He sent for Paloi the foreman and told him not to finish the room they were preparing for him. Paloi replied insolently that he took orders only from the Commune.

Every morning we went up to my father's room for breakfast. Then we came down to my mother's room and spent the day there. Every day we went for a walk in the garden as it was good for my brother's health. My father was almost always insulted by the guard.

Pétion sent a turnkey, Rocher, the horrible man who broke into my father's room and wanted to murder him during the riot at the Tuileries on 20th June 1792. This man was always in the tower and tried by every means to torment my father. Sometimes he sang the *Carmagnole* and other horrid songs, and sometimes, knowing that my father did not like the smell of a pipe, he would puff smoke at him as he passed. We had to pass through his room on the way to supper, and sometimes he was in bed. There was no sort of annoyance or insult which this man did not invent. My father bore it all very sweetly and forgave the man with all his heart.

My father was short of everything. He wrote to Pétion asking for the money for personal expenses, which he should have received, but there was no reply.

The garden was full of workmen who often insulted my father. There was one who boasted that he would strike my mother on the head with his tools. Pétion had him arrested.

The insults redoubled on the second of September.

That was the day the people learnt that Verdun had fallen to the invading armies. Frenzied and fearful, they sounded the tocsin and, as we heard later, posted up signs saying, "The people must themselves execute justice. Before we hasten to the frontier let us put bad citizens to death." The mob then acted on this, massacring the nobles, the relatives of emigrés, and the priests who would not obey the anti-religious orders of the Commune.

People threw stones from the windows at my father. Luckily, they did not hit him or anyone else. But there were a few who showed courage and sympathy. At another window a woman wrote on a square of cardboard, "Verdun is taken." She put it for a moment in the window and my aunt had time to read it. The municipal guards did not see her.

Hardly had we received this news when a fresh municipal guard called Mathieu arrived. He was inflamed with anger and told my father to go up to his room. We went with him as we were afraid they wanted to separate us. Mathieu then turned on my father and vented his rage upon him. Among other things, he said, "The drums have beaten the call to arms, the tocsin has sounded, the alarm gun has been fired, the enemy are at Verdun. If they come here we shall die, but you will be the first."

My father listened to these insults and countless others like them with the calm inspired by innocence. My brother burst into tears and ran into the other room. I had the greatest difficulty in consoling him. He already imagined our father dead.

The municipal guards all reproached Mathieu for his violence. All the same, they were no better disposed than he was. They told my father they were sure that the King of Prussia was marching against France and killing French soldiers under an order signed "Louis." My father was dreadfully upset by this slander and begged the municipal guards to contradict it outside.

My mother heard the drums beating the call to arms all night, but we did not know what was happening.

Marie Thérèse Charlotte and her brother Louis Charles, the Dauphin

Marie Thérèse Charlotte, called Madame Royale

Louis XVI and Marie Antoinette (Louis is 17 years old, Marie Antoinette is 15.)

King Louis XVI of France

Madame Elisabeth, sister of Louis XVI

The Royal Family

COMTE DE PROVENCE, LATER LOUIS XVIII, ELDER BROTHER OF LOUIS XVI

Comte d'Artois, younger brother of Louis XVI

THE PRINCESS DE LAMBALLE

THE ATTACK ON VERSAILLES

The last interview of Louis XVI with his family

Marie Antoinette in prison

THE SEPTEMBER MASSACRES

The next day at ten in the morning, Manuel came to see my father and assured him that Mme de Lamballe and the other persons who had been taken away from the Temple were all together at La Force prison and quite safe.

At three o'clock we heard fearful cries. As my father and mother left the dinner table to play backgammon, the principal guard, who behaved well, shut the door and windows and drew the curtains so that we should not see what was happening. That was right and proper.

The workmen in the Temple and Rocher, the turnkey, joined the murderers and the noise increased.

Several municipal guards and officers of the National Guard arrived. The latter wanted my father to show himself at the window. The municipality men very rightly objected.

When my father asked what was happening a young officer said to him, "Very well, sir, as you wish to know, the people outside want to show you the head of Mme de Lamballe."

My mother was frozen with horror. The men from the municipality scolded the officer, but my father, with his usual good nature, excused him by saying that it was his fault for having asked the officer, who had merely answered his question.

The din continued until five o'clock. We learnt afterwards that the crowd had wanted to break open the doors, but the municipal guards had prevented them by putting a tricolored sash on the gate. They had, however, allowed six of the assassins to walk around the tower carrying the head of Mme de Lamballe. The crowd wanted them to drag the body round, too, but they had to leave it at the door. When the deputation entered the Temple, Rocher uttered cries of joy on seeing the head of Mme de Lamballe, and scolded a young man who was sick with horror at the spectacle. It is said that a man was arrested later, accused of tearing the heart from the body, roasting it, and eating it.

Hardly was the rioting over when Pétion, who should have been occupied in putting a stop to the massacre, cooly sent his secretary to my father to count out some money for him. The municipal guard who had sacrificed his sash in putting it on the gate made my father pay him the cost of it.

My aunt and I heard them beating the call to arms all that night. We did not think that the massacre was still going on. My poor mother could not sleep that night. It was only later that we learnt that the massacre had lasted for three days, and that thousands, especially members of the clergy, had suffered terrible deaths.

One could not credit the extraordinary behavior of

the municipal men and guards; they seemed to be afraid of everything; a bad conscience, no doubt. One day, a man with a new gun fired it off outside to try it. They detained him and questioned him closely.

Another evening, at supper time, the call to arms was heard several times. The guards thought the foreigners had come, and that horrible Rocher took his great sabre and said to my father, "If they come here, I shall kill you." It turned out to be nothing but a misunderstanding between two patrols.

Another time a hundred workmen tried to force open the iron gates on the side of the Rotunda. The municipality men and the guard hurried there and dispersed them.

All these fears caused discipline to become stricter. Nevertheless, we found two of the municipals who alleviated my father's misery by showing him kindness and encouraging him to hope. I believe they are dead.

There was also a sentinel who had a conversation with my aunt through the keyhole. This poor fellow never ceased weeping all the time he was in the Temple. I don't know what has happened to him. May Heaven reward him for his loyalty to the King.

I studied the rules of arithmetic and copied out extracts from books with a municipal always looking over my shoulder, thinking that I was planning some sort of conspiracy.

They took away the newspapers from us, fearing that we should learn the news from abroad. But one day, full of glee, they brought one to my father, saying there was something interesting in it. What a horror! It said that they would put his head inside a red-hot cannon ball.

And one evening a municipal, on arrival, offered us

threats and insults, saying that we should all be killed if the enemy approached. He said the only one he was sorry for was my brother, but that, as he was born of a tyrant, he would have to die, too.

DEPRIVATIONS OF THE ROYAL FAMILY

This was the usual timetable of my august parents. My father got up at seven and prayed until eight, after which he dressed until nine, with my brother to keep him company. Then he went to breakfast with my mother.

After breakfast my father came down again with my brother to whom he gave lessons until eleven. Then my brother played until noon, after which we all went for a walk in the garden, whatever the weather, because the guard was relieved at this time and the new guard wished to see my father and bc sure that he was in the Temple.

Our walk lasted until two o'clock, when we dined. After dinner my father and mother played backgammon or picquet. At four my mother went up to her room with my brother, because my father generally slept then. At six my brother came down and my father gave him lessons, or played with him until supper.

At nine o'clock, immediately after supper, my mother

undressed my brother and put him to bed. She always heard his prayers before he went to sleep, and after that terrible thing happened to Mme de Lamballe my mother taught him to say a prayer especially for her and to ask God to protect the life of Mme de Tourzel, both of whom had had the goodness to accompany us to the Temple. If the municipals were near, he knew enough to do this in a low voice. Then we went upstairs again, as my father did not go to bed until eleven.

My mother's life was more or less the same as my father's. She worked a lot at her embroidery. My aunt often said prayers during the daytime; she always went through the service for the day, read many religious books, and spent much time in meditation. Like my father, she fasted on the days ordained by the Church.

The Republic had been established September twenty-second, we were told joyfully. We were also told of the departure of the foreign army; we could not believe it, but it was true.

At the beginning of October they took away our pens, paper, ink and pencils; they searched everywhere, and even harshly. This did not prevent my mother and me from hiding our pencils; my father and aunt gave up theirs.

The evening of the same day, as my father was finishing supper, they told him to wait, that he was going into another lodging in the Great Tower and would, in future, be separated from us. At this dreadful news my mother lost her usual courage.

We parted from him with many tears, still hoping, however, to see him again. The next day they brought our breakfast separately from his; my mother would eat nothing. The municipals, frightened and troubled by her gloomy grief, allowed us, then, to see my father, but only at meals. We were forbidden to speak in low tones or in foreign languages, only "aloud and in good French." This was undoubtedly aimed at my mother, to whom they referred as "The Austrian."

We went to dine with my father in great joy at seeing him again; but a municipal was there who, seeing that my aunt spoke low to my father, made a scene. Since my brother went to bed early, either my mother or my aunt stayed with him, while the other went with me to sup with my father.

Manuel came to see my father and harshly took away from him his *cordon rouge* (order of Saint-Louis) and assured him that none of those who had been at the Temple, excepting Mme de Lamballe, had perished. A municipal, coming in one evening, woke my brother roughly to see if he was still there; this was the only moment of anger I saw my mother show. Another municipal told my mother that it was not Pétion's purpose to have my father die, but to shut him up for life with my brother in the castle of Chambord. I do not know what object that man had in giving us this information; we never saw him again.

My father had Cléry, his valet, in his room at night as well as a municipal. The windows were secured by iron bars and shutters; the chimney smoked a lot.

The night we were taken from the Tuileries to the Assembly, Cléry, in pure terror, jumped from a window of the palace and hid out in the country. But when he heard of the arrest of my father, remorse overcame him and he had the courage to go to see Pétion and to ask permission to serve his King. This was granted, though they made him take an oath to be faithful to the nation.

We had no comfort now except our affection for one another. Even common necessities were denied us. The small stock of underwear lent to us by friends long gone was becoming worn, so my mother and aunt mended their clothes every day, and after my father had gone to bed, my aunt mended his. When some linen was finally sent, it was seen to have embroidered crowned letters and my mother and aunt were ordered to pick them out with their needles and scissors.

In November the whole family came down with colds and Cléry had an attack of rheumatic fever. On hearing this my aunt, though feverish herself, brought him cooling drinks, and my brother insisted on staying up to share a box of lozenges with him, although he could hardly keep his eyes open.

On 7th December a deputation from the Commune brought an order that the Royal Family should be deprived of "knives, scissors, pen-knives, and all other cutting instruments." My father gave up a knife, a pair of scissors and a pen-knife. The officials searched the rooms, taking away the little toilet implements of gold and silver and the working materials of my mother and aunt. Shortly after that, my aunt was mending my father's coat and she had to break a thread with her teeth.

My mother had to take on some of the duties of a servant. This was especially painful to my father. "Ah, what an employment for a Queen of France!" he once exclaimed. "Could they see that at Vienna! Who would have foreseen that, in uniting your lot to mine, you would have descended so low?"

"And do you esteem as nothing," my mother answered, "the glory of being the wife of one of the best and the most persecuted of men? Are not such misfortunes the noblest honors?"

TRIAL OF THE KING

The newspapers were returned to us in order that we might read of the departure of the foreigners and the horrible threats to the King.

For the first time members of the Convention came to see my father. They asked him if he had any complaints to make; he said no, that he was satisfied so long as he was with his family. They came back after dinner and asked him the same questions. The next day one of them, Drouet, came back alone and asked my mother if she had any complaints. She made him no answer.

The Commune changed on the second of December. The new municipal came to inspect my father and his family at ten o'clock that night. Some days later we were made very anxious by the beating of the drums and the arrival of a guard. At eleven o'clock Chambon and Chaumette, one the mayor, the other the public prosecutor of the Commune, and Colombeau, their clerk, went to my father's room. There they informed him of a decree of the Convention which ordered that he be brought to its bar to be interrogated. They then discovered that they did not have the decree with them, so they kept my father waiting two hours while they got it. They did not start out until one o'clock—the King in the mayor's carriage escorted by municipals on foot.

I shall not speak of my father's conduct before the Convention; all the world knows it—his firmness, his gentleness and kindness, his courage amid assassins thirsting for his blood; traits which will never be forgotten, and which the most remote posterity will admire.

The King, my father, returned at six o'clock. We had been in a state of anxiety impossible to express. My mother made every effort to learn from the municipals who guarded her what was happening; it was the first time that she deigned to question them. They would tell her nothing, and it was only after my father's return that we heard the facts. As soon as he returned she asked urgently to see him; she even sent to Chambon to ask it, but received no reply. She remained up all night in gloom so great that my aunt and I did not like to leave her, but she forced us to go to bed.

The next day she again asked to see my father and to read the journals to learn about his trial; she insisted that, if *she* could not see my father, at least permission should be granted to my brother and me. The request was taken to the council-general. The newspapers were refused, but we were permitted to see our father only on condition that *we should be absolutely separated from our mother.*

My father, on hearing of this, said that however great his pleasure might be in seeing his children, the serious business in which he was now engaged would not allow him to see his son, and that his daughter must not leave her mother.

My aunt resorted to desperate measures. Her room was directly under Cléry's, so at night messages were passed by means of a string let down from his room to hers and then drawn up again. She pricked a note on paper with a pin asking for a word from her brother's own hand. This secret communication was a great consolation to my father, though he warned Cléry that he was exposing himself to too much danger, that he should take care.

Other than through this, or through the municipals—and then with great difficulty—my father heard no news of us, nor we of him. He no longer went into the garden; neither did we. I had trouble in my foot and my father, hearing of it, grieved about it with his customary kindness and inquired about my condition.

My family found in this Commune a few charitable men who, out of sympathy, soothed our torture. They assured my mother that my father would not be put to death, that his case would be sent to the primary assemblies which would certainly save him. Alas, they deceived themselves, or from pity tried to deceive my mother.

On 26th December my father made his will because he fully expected to be murdered that day on his way to the bar of the Convention. He went there, however, with his usual calmness and courage, and left to his council the care of his defense. He went at eleven and returned at three. During that time they made him listen to the *acte enonciatif,* article by article: all sorts of false charges such as insults offered to the national cocarde, refusal to sanction the Declaration of Rights as well as several constitutional articles, practices to effect a counter-revolution, bribery, silence observed respecting the Treaty of Pilnitz, and organization of secret societies in Paris.

After each accusation, the President asked, "What have you to answer?" My father firmly denied the untruths and appealed to the Constitution from which he declared he had never swerved. His answers were very gentle, but on the charge, "You spilt the blood of the people on the tenth of August," he, who had always been so careful lest the blood of a Frenchman be spilt, exclaimed with emphasis, "No, sir, no: it was not I!"

We learnt that all this time he had not had anything to eat and this, with all the strain of the questioning he had undergone, made him stagger from weakness. Someone asked him if he wished some refreshment; he refused. But a moment after, seeing a grenadier of the escort offer a companion half of his small loaf of bread, the King asked him in a whisper if he might have a piece.

"Ask aloud for what you want," said the man roughly, as if he feared being suspected of pity.

"I asked you for a piece of your bread," my father said.

This seemed to touch the man, for he replied, "Divide it with me. It is a Spartan breakfast. If I had a root, I would give you half."

This was the only kindness shown my father, the King, that day.

DEATH OF THE KING

On 18th January 1793, the day on which the verdict was given, the municipals entered my father's room at eleven o'clock, saying they had orders not to let him out of their sight. He asked if his fate had been decided; they answered, "No." But the next morning faithful old M. de Malesherbes, a former Court councillor who had been granted access to the King, came to tell him that his sentence had been pronounced. "But Sire," he added, in tears, "those wretches are not yet masters; all honest men will now come forward to save Your Majesty or perish at your feet."

"Old friend," said my father, "that would compromise many persons and start civil war in France. I would rather die. I beg you to order them for me to make no attempt to save me; the King does not die in France."

After this my father was not allowed to see his council; he sent a note asking for that privilege and complaining of the restraint he was under in being watched incessantly. No attention was paid.

Sunday the twentieth, the minister of justice came with twelve to fifteen men—the Executive Council—to notify the King that his sentence of death would be executed the next day. Garat, the Minister of Justice, wearing his hat, acted as spokesman. "Louis," he said, "the National Convention has instructed the Executive Council to signify to you its decree of the 15th, 16th, 17th, 19th, and 20th of January. The Secretary of the Council will read them to you."

The man stepped forward and read that the National Convention declared "Louis Capet," last King of France, guilty of conspiracy against the liberty of the nation and attempting to undermine the safety of the State; the National Convention decreed that Louis Capet should suffer the death penalty. They said that he would be put to death within twenty-four hours.

My father asked a respite of three days to find out what would become of his family and to arrange for a Catholic confessor. The respite was refused. He was assured that there was no charge against his family and that they would all be sent out of the country. He asked for his confessor, Abbé Edgeworth de Firmont, and gave the Abbé's address. After they left, my father dined as usual, which surprised the municipals, who expected that he would want to kill himself. Then he went to bed and to sleep.

That day the rest of us learned from the street-vendors of my father's sentence of death.

At seven in the evening we were informed that an order from the Convention authorized us to go to my father. We ran to his room and found him very much changed. He wept for our grief, but not on account of his own death. He told my mother the story of his trial, making excuses for his murderers. Then he gave my brother some good religious advice, and told him in particular to forgive the people who had ordered his death. He gave his blessing to my brother and me.

My mother was very anxious for us to spend the night with my father but he refused as he needed to be quiet. She asked leave to return to him next morning. He agreed to this, but after we had gone away he asked the guards to see that we did not come again because it caused him too much pain.

That evening my mother scarcely had strength to undress my brother and put him to bed. She threw herself, dressed as she was, upon the bed and we heard her throughout the night shuddering with cold and with sorrow.

The morning of that terrible day, 21st January 1793, we rose at six o'clock. At a quarter past six they opened our door to look for a prayer book for my father's Mass. We thought we were to go to him, and we still had that hope until the roll of the drums and the cries of joy of a frenzied populace came, and we knew that the crime had been done.

In the afternoon my mother asked to see Cléry, who had been with my father until the time he left for the scaffold. She thought that he had, perhaps, entrusted him with a message for her. My father had, in fact, charged Cléry with returning his wedding ring to my mother, adding that he parted from it only in parting with life. He also gave him a packet of my mother's hair, and ours, saying that they had been so dear to him that he had kept them until the last instant. But the municipals refused to let Cléry see us. We heard that Cléry was in despair because of this. My mother then asked that her request to see Cléry be made to the council general; she also asked for mourning clothes.

We were allowed to see the persons who brought our mourning clothes, but only in the presence of the municipals. My mother would no longer go down in the garden because this obliged her to pass the door of my father's room, which pained her too much. But fearing that want of air might harm my brother and myself, in February she asked to go up on the tower, which was granted to her.

On the twentieth, at half past ten at night, my mother and I had just gone to bed when several municipals arrived. We rose hastily. They read us a decree of the Convention ordering that we should be carefully searched, even to the mattresses. My poor brother was asleep; they roughly pulled him out of his bed to search it. My mother held him, all shivering with cold and fear. They took from my mother the address of a shop she had always kept, a stick of sealing wax from my aunt, and from me a Sacred Heart of Jesus scapular and a prayer for France. Their search did not end until four in the morning. They wrote a *procès-verbal* of all they found and obliged my mother and aunt to sign it, threatening to carry off my brother and me if they refused. They were furious at having found nothing but trifles.

Three days later they returned, and demanded to see my aunt in private. They then questioned her about a man's hat they had found in her room. They wished to know whence it came, how long she had had it, and why she had kept it. She answered that it had belonged to her brother at the beginning of his imprisonment in the Temple and that she had asked to keep it for love of him.

The municipals said that it was a suspicious thing and should be taken away. My aunt insisted on keeping it but was not allowed to do so. They forced her to sign her answer, and they carried away the hat.

THE LITTLE KING IS TAKEN AWAY

One night my brother felt very ill, so they sent for a surgeon called Soupé and a truss-fitter named Pipelet to bandage him for hernia.

Mme Tison (the wife of the jailer) went out of her mind. She was very upset by my brother's illness and tormented by remorse. She had been unwell for a long time. After a time she would not go out into the air, and then she began to talk to herself. Unfortunately that made me laugh, and my poor mother—and my aunt, as well—looked at me kindly, as though my laughter did them good. Mme Tison kept talking about her sins and the ruin of her family, as well as about prison and the scaffold. She thought that the persons she had denounced had been killed. Every evening she waited to see whether the municipal guards she had denounced would come or not. When she did not see them, she went to bed and had terrible dreams, which made her worse.

My mother and aunt could not have been kinder to this woman, though they had no reason to be grateful to her. They nursed her and encouraged her all the time she was in the Temple.

One day the municipals took her from the tower and put her in the castle. Then, as her madness got worse, they placed her in the hospital and put a woman spy along with her to question her on behalf of the government. The municipals asked us to send some linen to this woman who had looked after our linens when she was with us.

On 3rd July, at ten o'clock at night, they read to us a decree issued by the Convention saying that my brother would be separated from my mother and placed in the safest room in the tower. As soon as my brother heard this he started screaming and threw himself into my mother's arms, begging not to be parted from her.

My mother, too, was horrified by this cruel order and would not give him up. She defended his bed against the municipals. But they insisted on taking him, and threatened to use violence and to send for the guard to carry him off by force.

An hour was spent in discussion and arguments, insults and threats by the municipals, and tears and opposition from all of us. At last my mother consented to give up her son. We got him up, and when he was dressed my mother handed him over to the municipals. She bathed him in tears, as if she foresaw that she would never see him again.

The poor little fellow kissed us all tenderly and departed in tears with the men.

My mother told the municipals before they went to ask the general council, urgently, to give her leave to see her son, if only at mealtimes. They undertook to do this.

My mother felt the height of unhappiness in being separated from him. However, she thought he was being looked after by an honest and educated man. Her misery increased when she knew that the shoemaker, Simon, whom she had known as a municipal, was in charge of her unhappy child.

My mother repeatedly asked for permission to see him, but did not receive it. Meanwhile, my brother cried inconsolably for two whole days and begged to see us.

THE QUEEN IS REMOVED TO THE CONCIERGERIE

The municipals no longer remained in my mother's room; we were locked in, day and night. The guards came only three times a day to bring our meals and to examine the bars of the windows to see if they were in order. We often went up to the tower. My brother went up every day, and the only pleasure my mother had was to watch him going by through a little window. Sometimes she waited for hours to get a glimpse of her darling child.

My mother got a little news of him from the municipals and from Tison, who went down on washing days, saw Simon and heard from him how he was. Tison tried to make amends for his bad conduct; he behaved better and gave my mother some news of her son, but not much.

Simon treated him very badly when he cried at being separated from us till at last the child was so frightened that he did not dare to weep.

The Convention heard a false report that my brother

had been seen on the boulevards and, learning that the guards were grumbling because they never saw him and said he was no longer in the Temple, they had him sent down to the garden so that people might see him.

Henriot, a new general, also came to see us. His rough manners astonished us. From the moment he came in to the moment he left he used bad language.

On 2nd August, at two in the morning, they came and woke us up to read a decree from the Convention ordering that, on the demand of the prosecutor of the Commune, my mother should be taken to the Conciergerie for trial.

My mother heard this order without flinching. My aunt and I immediately asked to be allowed to go with her, but, as the decree did not call for this, they refused.

My mother packed up her clothes in a bundle. The municipals did not leave her and she was obliged to dress in front of them. They asked for her handbags which she gave them. They went through them, took out whatever was inside—though there was nothing of any importance—and made a parcel of the contents which they said would be opened by the tribunal in the presence of my mother. They left her only a handkerchief and a bottle of smelling salts in case she felt unwell.

At last my mother went, after embracing me and telling me to be brave and to look after my health. I did not reply. I was quite sure that I would never see her again.

My mother had to stop at the bottom of the tower while the municipals drew up a paper for her discharge from the Temple. As she went out she knocked her head against the lintel of the door, which was lower than she thought, but she did not hurt herself very much. One of the men asked her if she was hurt. "No," she replied, "nothing can hurt me now." After that she got into a carriage with a municipal and two constables.

Several days later, my mother sent for her things. She asked for her knitting, which she was very fond of, as she was knitting a pair of stockings for my brother. We sent it to her, but heard afterwards that it had not been delivered for fear that she should harm herself with the needles.

At first we heard little news of my brother from the municipals, but that did not last long. Every day we heard him singing with Simon the *Carmagnole* and the *Marseillaise,* and many other horrid songs. Simon made him wear a red bonnet and a carmagnole jacket and forced him to sing at the windows so as to be heard by the guard, and to utter fearful blasphemies against God and to curse his family and the aristocrats. My mother happily did not hear all these horrors, for she had already gone.

After her departure they came to look for my brother's colored clothes. My mother had said she hoped he would continue to wear mourning, but the first thing Simon did was to take off his black suit.

The change in the manner of his life and the ill-treatment he suffered made my brother ill at the end of August. Simon gave him horrible food and made him drink a lot of wine, which he detested. All that made him feverish. They gave him some medicine which did no good and which disturbed his health. He got very fat but did not grow in height. However, Simon made him go for walks and take the air on the roof of the tower.

My aunt and I were inconsolable, and we passed many days and nights in tears. However, when my mother was taken, they had assured my aunt that no harm would come to her. It was a great consolation for me not to be parted from my aunt, whom I loved much; but, alas, all is now changed, and I have lost her, too.

INTERROGATION OF THE PRINCESSES

At the beginning of September I was upset and worried about my mother; every time I heard the drums beat I feared another second of September massacre.

We spent the month quietly enough, however, going up on the roof every day. The municipals visited us punctually three times a day, but their strictness did not prevent us from getting news, particularly of my mother, about whom we were anxious.

We learnt that she was accused of writing to people outside, so at once we threw away the writing materials and pencils that we had managed to keep in spite of the searches. We feared they would make us undress before Mme Simon and that if the things were found they might compromise my mother. We also learnt that my mother had thought of escaping, and that the wife of the jailer was kind and was taking care of her. Afterwards, we learnt that this woman had been questioned secretly, but we did not know about what.

The municipals came again to ask for underlinen for my mother, but they would not give us any news of her health. They took away the embroidery we were doing, as they feared it consisted of magical and dangerous characters.

My aunt and I did not know if my mother was alive or dead. There were times when we were full of apprehension for her, seeing the rage of the people against her. Though we heard a street-seller cry out that they wanted her trial to take place without any interruption, hope, the natural consoler of the wretched, made us believe that she would be saved.

We could not picture to ourselves the unworthy conduct of the Emperor of Austria who left the Queen, his kinswoman, to perish on the scaffold, without doing anything to save her. But that is what happened.

My aunt talked of my father often. She said that he had had such good intentions and desired so much to make his people happy, and that he was very good and very superior to the whole Court united; but that he feared making a mistake and was tormented by the dread of doing injustice, and that from the integrity of his own nature he could not see the evil in others.

The searches began again, and we were treated harshly. My aunt, who had a sore on her arm, had great difficulty in getting something to treat it with. They kept her waiting a long time. At last one of the municipals protested against the inhumanity of this behavior and sent for some ointment.

In order to treat us still more harshly we were deprived of whatever was convenient, for example, of the armchair used by my aunt. They also took away my herb tea which my aunt insisted I drink every morning for my health. We could not even have what was necessary.

When our meals were brought now, they were passed through a wicket that had been installed in our entrance door, and the wicket was closed quickly so that we might not see who brought them. We made our own beds and were obliged to sweep the floor, which took us a long time at first because we were not used to it. We no longer had anyone to wait on us. The public prosecutor, Hébert, said to my aunt that equality was the first law of the French Republic and, as no other persons detained in prison had servants, he was taking away Tison.

We still could get no news of my mother, except by listening to the street-crier, but that was very indistinct, although we listened with all our might. We were forbidden to go up on the tower for air, and they took away our large sheets under the pretext that, despite the thick bars, we should get down from the window. They brought us coarse and dirty blankets.

At noon, on 8th October, when my aunt and I were setting our room to rights and dressing ourselves, three members of the Convention, Pache, Chaumette and David, arrived with several municipals.

My aunt did not open the door until she was dressed. Pache, turning to me, asked me to go downstairs. My aunt tried to follow me, but was prevented. She asked whether I would come up again. Chaumette assured her of it, saying, "You may rely on the word of a good republican; she will come up." I embraced my aunt, who was trembling all over, and I went down. I was very embarrassed. It was the first time I was ever alone with men. I did not know what they wanted, but I commended myself to God.

I found my brother there also, and I embraced him tenderly; but they tore him out of my arms and told me to go into the other room. Chaumette made me sit down, then he placed himself opposite me. He and Hébert questioned me about a number of villainous things of which my mother and my aunt were accused. I was overwhelmed by such horror and so offended that, in spite of the fear I felt, I could not help saying that it was infamous. There were some things which I did not understand; but what I did understand was so horrible that I wept with indignation.

They questioned me about Varennes, too, and put many questions to me, to which I replied as best I could without compromising anybody. I had always heard my parents say that it was better to die than to compromise anyone whomsoever.

At last, at three o'clock, my examination ended; it had begun at noon. I begged Chaumette to let me rejoin my mother.

"I can do nothing about it," he said to me.

"Can you not get permission from the council-general?'

"I have no authority there."

He then had three municipals take me back to my room, advising me to say nothing to my aunt, who was also to go downstairs. I threw myself into her arms, but they separated us and made her go down. She came up again at four o'clock. Her examination had lasted only one hour, and mine three. That was because the deputies saw that they could not intimidate her as they hoped to do to a person of my age; but the life I had led these last years, and the example of my parents, had given me strength to withstand them.

THE LITTLE KING'S ILL TREATMENT

The winter passed quietly enough and we were given some wood for our fire. There were many visits and searches. One of the searches lasted for hours, and ended only at half-past eight at night. I asked my aunt what they were so persistently searching for, and she said they thought that my mother and she had hidden their diamonds some place there. The four municipals who made the search were drunk. I cannot give you an idea of their talk, the rudeness and the bad language during all that time.

They took away a lot of silly things like hats, playing cards with kings on them, and books with the royal arms. They left us our religious books, after hurling many insults at our religion.

Simon accused us of making false money—*assignats*—and of corresponding with the outside world. He insisted that we had corresponded with my father during his trial. He made a statement to this effect in the name of my brother, and he forced him to sign it. The noise, which he believed was made by us coining money, was the sound of tric-trac, a game that we used to play in the evenings.

On 19th January 1794 we heard a great noise from my brother's room, from which we guessed he was being taken away from the Temple. We felt this was so when, looking through the shutters, we saw a lot of parcels being carried away. During the following days, we heard his door being opened and believed they had taken him away and put some foreign or German prisoner in his room. We felt the need to give this unknown prisoner a name, so we called him Melchizedek. I learnt afterwards that it was only Simon who had gone away. He had been given the choice of becoming a municipal guard or staying with my brother, and he had chosen to become a guard. So now my poor little brother was left quite alone.

I think it unheard of savagery to leave an unhappy child of eight alone, locked in a room behind bolts and bars, with no one to help him, and with only an inefficient bell which he never pulled, as he preferred to go without things rather than ask his persecutors for them.

We heard later that his bed was not made for six months, as my brother was not strong enough to make it. He was covered with bugs and fleas which swarmed on his body and in his clothes. His wastes remained in his room. He never threw them out, nor did anyone else. The window was never opened and the smell of the room was unendurable. By nature my brother was inclined to be dirty and idle, and did not take care of his person as he should have.

Often they gave him no light. The poor boy was frightened to death, but he never asked for anything. He spent the day doing nothing, and the wretched existence he led had a bad effect on his moral and physical welfare.

During Lent, they no longer gave my aunt fish on fast days. She asked to be given fast-day dishes so that she could do her duty. This was refused on the ground of equality. It was pointed out that there was no difference in the days, that there were no longer weeks, but periods of ten days. They brought us an almanac, but we did not look at it. Another day, when my aunt asked for Lenten-fare, they said to her, "But, citizeness, you don't know what is happening. One can't get everything one wants in the market." After that my aunt asked no more. She kept the whole Lent though. She ate no breakfast; at dinner she took a bowl of coffee with milk (it was her breakfast which she kept over), and in the evening she ate nothing but bread. She bade me eat whatever they brought me, as I had not reached the prescribed age for abstinence.

At the beginning of spring they took away our candle, and we went to bed when we could no longer see.

DEATH OF PRINCESS ELISABETH

On 9th May, just as we were going to bed, the bolts outside were drawn and there was a knock at our door. My aunt said that she would put on her dress; they replied that they could not wait so long and knocked so hard one would think they were breaking in the door. She opened it to them when she was dressed. They said to her, "Citizeness, be so good as to come downstairs."

"And my niece . . . my little girl?"

"She will be attended to afterwards."

My aunt embraced me and to calm me said she would be coming up again.

"No, citizeness," one of them answered, "you are *not* coming up again; take your cap and go down."

Then they heaped insults and rude remarks on her. She endured them patiently, put on her cap, kissed me again and told me to preserve courage and firmness, to hope in God always, to profit by the good religious principles my parents had given me, and not to fail to observe the last injunctions of my father and mother. She went out. On arriving below she was made to empty her pockets which had nothing in them. The municipals took a long time drawing up a report to discharge them of responsibility for her person.

I had no way of knowing then that after many insults she was made to appear before the Revolutionary Tribunal; that the Tribunal said that it was to the family of the Capets (that is what they called us) that the French people owed all the evils under which they had groaned for so many centuries; that she was condemned to die; that she was taken to the Conciergerie and that she asked to spend her last night with twenty-four others who were waiting to die because she wished to comfort them. They made her wait till the last, nearest the steps of the scaffold, and watch the others die, which she did without flinching, comforting the others to the end. After they had all been murdered they were stripped naked because it was said that their clothes belonged to the State. I think my aunt would have minded that more than being killed, for she was very modest.

22

MADAME ROYALE ALONE

I was left in great desolation when I found myself separated from my aunt; no one would tell me what had become of her. I spent a very wretched night, and yet, although I was very anxious about her fate, I was far from believing that I was to lose her in a few hours. Sometimes I persuaded myself that she was to be sent away from France; but when I remembered how they had taken her all my fears returned.

The next day I asked the municipal officers what had become of her; they said she had gone to take the air. I renewed my request to rejoin my mother since I was separated from my aunt, and they answered that they would talk about it.

They came afterwards to bring me the key of the wardrobe containing my aunt's linen. I asked to send her some, as she had none; they told me it could not be done.

Remembering that my aunt had told me that if ever I

was alone it would be my duty to ask for a woman to keep me company, I did so out of obedience, but with repugnance, feeling sure that I would either be refused or be given some vile woman. In fact, when I did make this request to the municipals they told me it was unnecessary.

They redoubled their severity and took away the knives they had given back, saying, "Tell me, citizeness, have you many knives?"

"No, gentlemen, only two."

"And have you none in your dressing-case, nor any scissors?"

"No, gentlemen."

Another time they took away my tinder-box; having found the fireplace hot, they said, "Might one know why you made a fire?"

"To put my feet in hot water." (I had been suffering from bad circulation in my foot.)

"What did you light the fire with?"

"With the tinder-box."

"Who gave it to you?"

"I do not know."

"Precisely; we are going to take it away from you. We do it for your own good, lest you fall asleep and burn yourself near the fire. You have nothing else?"

"No, gentlemen."

Such visits and scenes were frequent. Except when I was definitely questioned I never spoke, not even to those who brought my food.

One day a man came; I think it was Robespierre. I had heard that he was one of the leaders of the Revolution. The municipals showed him great respect; I did not speak. His visit was a secret to the people in the tower, who either did not know who he was or were unwilling to tell me. He only looked at me insolently, glanced over my books and, after searching with the municipals, left.

Religion was my only consolation. I had kept my aunt's book of devotions; I read them, I recalled her councils, and tried to follow them exactly. With respect for my aunt's wishes, I asked again for a woman. They again refused, and I was glad of it. I asked if I could take care of my brother and they refused.

My aunt, who had foreseen only too clearly the misfortunes in store for me, had accustomed me to wait on myself and to need no assistance. She had so regulated my life that every hour was occupied: the care of my room, prayer, reading, work—all had their own time. She had taught me to make my bed alone, to comb my hair and dress myself—things that formerly had been done for me. Moreover, she had neglected nothing which would contribute to my health. She made me sprinkle water about so as to freshen the air of my room; and she also made me walk very fast for an hour, with a watch in my hand, in order to prevent stagnation of the blood.

My brother was still wallowing in filth; no one entered his room except at meal times; no one had any pity on that unfortunate child, nor were we allowed to see each other.

I asked for nothing but mere necessities. Sometimes they were rudely refused. But I could, at least, keep myself clean; I had soap and water. I swept the room every day; I had it done by nine o'clock when they came to bring me my breakfast. I had no lights but in the long days I suffered less from this privation. They would no longer give me books; I had only the religious ones and some travels, which I read a thousand times. I also had some knitting which bored me dreadfully.

One day I heard the general alarm beaten and I was so filled with loneliness I hoped it meant death for me, for I have no fear of death and any change would have been better than my present existence. I must have fainted, for I awoke as from a deep, deep sleep, without any idea of how long I had been unconscious. I said to myself, "If they should end by putting any person with me who is not a monster, I feel that I could not help but love her." In my desperation I scratched upon the wall:

Marie Thérèse is the most unhappy creature in the world. She can obtain no news of her mother; nor be reunited to her, though she has asked it for a thousand times.

Live, my good mother! whom I love well, but of whom I can hear no tidings.

O my father! watch over me from heaven above.

O my God! forgive those who have made my family die.

A YOUNG GUARDIAN

At six in the morning, the 28th July, I heard a frightful noise at the Temple: the guard called to arms, the drums rolled and the doors opened and closed. All this racket was caused by a visit from certain members of the National Assembly who came to assure themselves that all was quiet. I heard the bolts of my brother's room drawn; I sprang out of bed and was dressed by the time the members reached my room.

They were in full dress, which astonished me because I was not used to seeing them so. A man called Barras talked to me familiarly, calling me by name. He was surprised to see me up and said several things to me. I made no answer. When they went I heard them haranguing the guards under the window, telling them to be faithful to the National Convention. There were shouts of "Long live the Republic!" and "Long live the National Convention!" The guard was doubled.

Next evening when I was in bed without any light, but not asleep because I was so anxious about what was going on, someone knocked on my door to show me to Laurent, a young commissioner of the Convention, who had been given charge of my brother and me. I rose and these men made a thorough search, showing Laurent everything. Then they left.

The following morning at ten o'clock, Laurent came alone and asked me politely if I needed anything. He came three times a day, always behaving with civility. He never searched the bureaus, either. I soon asked him for what interested me most keenly, news of my loved ones. I also asked to be reunited with my mother. He answered, with a very sad expression, that this was not within his power.

The next day some men in tricolor sashes came and I put the same question to them. They answered that they did not understand why I did not want to remain here because it seemed to them that I was very well off.

"It is frightful," I told them, "to be separated from my mother for a year without learning any news of her, or of my aunt, either."

"You are not ill, citizeness?"

"No, gentlemen, but heart sickness is the most cruel of all."

"I tell you," said one roughly, "we can do nothing about it; but my advice to you is to be patient, and to hope in the justice and goodness of the French people."

I said nothing more.

Another winter passed. I was satisfied with the civility of these guardians; they wished to make my fire and gave me all the wood I wanted, which pleased me, for my hands had become swollen with chilblains from having been blue with cold. They also brought me the books I asked for; Laurent had already given me some.

I have nothing but praise for his manner during the whole time he was in attendance. He often asked me if I needed anything. He begged me to tell him what I would like and told me to ring whenever I needed something. He gave me back my tinder-box and candle, and even made me gifts of such luxuries as hair powder, tea, and orange-flower water. He was twenty-four and handsome. Still, my greatest grief was that I could get no news of my mother and aunt; I dared not ask, but I thought of them constantly.

At the end of March I was disturbed to find that Laurent had been replaced by Lasne, a former house painter. But he, too, seemed to have a kind heart; he even invited me to go up to the top of the tower to get some air.

One day in June the door opened and a lady in her early thirties entered, trembling and weeping. She said she was Mme Chantereine, my appointed companion. She was not a Court lady but the daughter of a ship-owner who had lost a fortune in these troubled times. She had been brought up in good provincial society, could speak Italian, and was a skilled embroideress. She was shocked to see me in my shabby, outgrown gray cotton dress, darned stockings and worn-out shoes. Since she was authorized to get some new clothes for me, she lost no time in ordering a splendid new wardrobe: two housecoats of colored taffeta, two of striped cotton lined with silk, six pairs of shoes, six pairs of colored silk stockings, two dozen linen chemises, and a gown of silk. I was even allowed paper, ink, chalks, paints and brushes, and new books, though they had to be approved. She arranged, also, to have the cleaning and laundry done.

All of this pleased me, but every day I asked to see my brother and asked for news of my mother and aunt. Mme Chantereine would give me no answer. Instead she got permission for us to walk in the Temple gardens. It was a great treat to again see trees and grass, to feel the sunshine, and to smell the flowers.

HEARTBREAK AND JOY

In the month of September 1795 Mme de Tourzel, my old governess, was authorized to pay me a visit. I could hardly believe it when Mme Chantereine, or Rennette, as I now called her, told me the good news. At the end of July, Rennette had reported to the Committee of Public Safety her high opinion of me. But my joy on seeing such an old friend was extinguished just before her visit when Rennette broke into tears and told me my mother and aunt no longer existed. I fell back upon my bed, speechless, gasping for breath. Then I cried until I could cry no more.

She did not tell me, as I have since discovered, that my mother's trial lasted three days and three nights without stopping; that they asked her questions such as, What had she done with her diamonds, and made shameful accusations; that she did not have the consolation of the last rites of the Church, as had my father; that they sent her a secular priest she considered no priest at all; that she knelt down alone for a long time, coughed a little, and then lay down. But the next morning, knowing that the rector of Sainte-Marguerite was imprisoned opposite, she went to her window, looked at the window in his cell, and knelt down. I am told that he gave her absolution and his blessing.

Nor did she tell me that my mother, the Queen of France, had not even been afforded the privilege of being driven in a carriage to her death, as had been my father, the King. They tied her hands behind her back and put her in an open cart to be reviled and spat upon, which she ignored with triumphant dignity.

Mme de Tourzel brought her daughter, Pauline, with her. Pauline and I had been playmates throughout childhood. Her mother had even taken her along with us when we were first confined here, and for that they had been imprisoned in the dreaded La Force prison. It was a tearful reunion for the three of us.

After we had recovered, Mme de Tourzel remarked on the change in me. She said that when she had last seen me I had been frail and delicate-looking, but now, in spite of all I had been through, I had grown strong and tall. And she said she was struck by my mingled likeness to my father, mother and aunt. That pleased me very much.

Mme de Tourzel waited until Rennette had left the room, and then gave me a letter she had secretly received in July from my uncle, the Comte de Provence:

> *I risk this letter, my dear niece, without knowing if it can reach you; but my affection for you can no longer remain silent at so sad a time. Nothing can make good the terrible losses that*

we have suffered; but let me try to temper their bitterness. Think of me, I implore you, as your father, and be very sure that I love you and will always love you as tenderly as if you were my own daughter. If those who bring you this letter can find means that allow you to reply in safety, I shall be delighted to hear that your heart accepts what mine offers. But in God's name commit no imprudence, and remember that your safety is far more important than my satisfaction. Farewell, my dear niece, I love you and embrace you with all my heart.

Although I had not seen my uncle since he emigrated, I remembered our family life together at Versailles. In a rush of feeling, while Mme de Tourzel and Pauline occupied the attention of Rennette, I dashed off this answer:

My dear uncle, I am more touched than I can say by the sentiments which you design to feel for an unhappy orphan, in wishing to adopt her as your daughter. The first real moment of joy that I savor for three years is that in which you assure me of your good will. I will always love you, and hope one day to assure you myself, of my gratitude and my affection. I am anxious for your health and to know what has happened to you in the three years since I had the pleasure of seeing you. I hope you are well. I pray for it every day and that Heaven may grant you long life and happiness, which may perhaps not be yours for a long time. Farewell: be sure that whatever hap-

pens I shall be attached to you till my last breath.

Marie Thérèse Charlotte

The Tourzels were permitted only two visits every ten days, although they wanted to come every day. After their first visit I wrote Pauline:

My dear Pauline,—The pleasure of seeing you has helped greatly to sooth my sorrow. During the long time that I was separated from you my thoughts dwelt often with you. To the sufferings I had to endure, anxiety while you were in gaol was added; I was thankful when I learnt that you were free, and I trusted you would never return to prison. My hopes were in vain; you were thrust into a second dungeon, where you languished even longer than in the first. At last you are safe. I did not hear of your second captivity until you had left the Palais Royal; since then you have endeavored to share mine, or at least to see me. Had I not already known and cared for you as I did, these further marks of the devotion you lavished upon my parents and myself would have served to attach me to you for life. Measure, then, by the tenderness of my former affection for you, the love I now bear you. I do love you, and shall continue to do so all my life.

Written at the Tower of the Temple, this sixth of September.

Marie Thérèse Charlotte

No one told me that the reasons I was now allowed visitors and better living conditions were that Robespierre had himself been guillotined and that the Reign of Terror was over. Public feeling had changed so that people were now beginning to take an interest in me. The wife of my father's former valet and one of our maids applied for permission to come and wait on me. My former sub-governess, Mme de Mackau, who had also taken care of my aunt, arrived. She was aged, and weakened from long imprisonment for having served the Royal Family, so I helped her around the garden and shielded her from the sun. Added to my friends were a tame goat that followed me around and a puppy named Coco that Laurent had given me before he went away.

In June I was told that my poor little brother had died. I learnt that his knees and wrists swelled so that it was feared that he was growing rickety, and during the winter he had had several attacks of fever though he huddled by the fire to keep warm. His illness increased and his knees swelled very much. He would not walk; still less would he go up to the tower for air. They made him take bad-tasting medicines, which he swallowed with difficulty. Happily, his malady did not make him suffer much; it was a total wasting away, rather than acute pain. Fever consumed him; he grew weaker daily, and finally he just closed his eyes and died. This unhappy child had long been given none but the worst treatment—and I believe that no record can show such barbarity to any other child.

On the eighth of November the Tourzels failed to arrive for their visit. It seems that their correspondence with my uncle had been reported, by whom I do not know; their house had been searched, they had been imprisoned again, and further visits to the Temple were forbidden.

I was plunged into gloom, but suddenly news of a different sort was brought to me. Negotiations had taken place for my exchange for a number of important Austrian-held French prisoners. I was to be handed over to my relatives in Austria who had so basely ignored the cruel fate of their own close relation, my mother the Queen, and her family.

It now seemed that my inheritance, whatever money or gold had been saved and the personal jewelry my mother sent out of the country before we started for Varennes, was in the hands of Austria. They thought it might be politic to marry me to one of the archdukes. This idea did not please me at all, and I resolved to resist it at all costs.

By now I think the people of Paris were beginning to feel a little sorry for me, and I guess I had become an embarrassment to the Convention; they must have thought it would be a good thing to get rid of me. Since the death of my brother, my uncle the Comte de Provence, being my father's eldest brother and natural successor, had assumed the title of King Louis XVIII. This did not bother me as, under the Salic law, I, a daughter, was excluded from ascending the throne of France or of claiming any land. Acting the part of a father, he, too, offered me protection and suggested that I marry my cousin the Duc d'Angoulême, son of his brother, the Comte d'Artois. Although I was not enthusiastic about marrying anyone, this met with my favor; he, at least, had been a member of our family, and this alliance had already been mentioned to my parents some years before.

Thus, even as my mother before me, I became a

pawn between France and Austria. I understand that some emigrés even urged that I should be kidnapped and conducted forthwith to my uncle, the King. The Emperor of Austria met this threat with one of his own; he ordered that no person be allowed to approach me once I started my journey.

The Committee of Public Safety proposed the exchange and the Convention signed the decree on 30th July 1795; but, with all the bickering and politicking, the final order to leave was not given until Friday, 27th November. Emperor Francis II of Austria had accepted the proposal of the Convention for the prisoner exchange, rather than for the large ransom he had first offered.

M. Benezech, Minister of the Interior, and, I am glad to say, a royalist at heart, was put in charge. He came to pay his respects—a proud old man—and to ask me which persons I would like to accompany us.

Whom should I choose? Of course, Mme de Tourzel was the first to come to my mind. And then, old and frail as she was, dear Mme de Mackau, and the wives of M. Huë and M. Turgot, both of whom had been in my father's service. Although Mme de Tourzel had been released from prison after a very brief stay, they refused to approve her appointment. Mme de Mackau felt too old and ill to undertake such a journey and begged that Mme de Soucy, her daughter, take her place. I consented, although I was not too fond of Mme de Soucy. Fancy, she took her son and her maid with her, while *I* was refused a serving-woman—such bad form! She is definitely not the person I should have selected.

I asked, also, for Mme de Sérent who had been one of my aunt's ladies. It was agreed, too, that I should have one of the commissioners from the Temple and a "respectable" police officer. I asked for M. Gomin from the Temple, for I understood that he had devotedly watched over my brother in his dying days. Faithful Huë and our old cook Meunier were added.

On 18th December 1795 M. Benezech and an aide came late at night and took over "the responsibility for Madame Royale."

They had given me quite a trousseau, about which I cared little, but I gathered together a few cherished things they had let me keep—my brother's backgammon board, a watch that had belonged to my grandmother, the Empress of Austria, and my dog Coco.

I bade Rennette farewell and we started to leave; but at the door I turned, and she looked so sad that I ran back to kiss her once more.

No one was in sight when we reached the frozen street. I was shivering, but not from the cold, as I paused for a last look at the sinister dark tower wherein I had shed so many tears and suffered such bitter anguish. I had lived there for three years, four months and five days. The clocks of Paris struck midnight as I stepped into the carriage that would carry me to a new life.

It was my seventeenth birthday.

EPILOGUE: MADAME ROYALE'S DESTINY

What more can be said of Madame Royale, Marie Thérèse Charlotte of France?

Only that, as she traveled further and further from the scene of all her sorrows, she began to experience something that she never thought possible again: she began to feel *young*! The air of freedom was seeping into her very bones and, with her troubles fading into the distance, a sensation of heady excitement—and a touch of the cockiness natural to youth—seemed to be taking hold. She was opening up to the outside world so long denied her as a flower opens to the sun; she was marching trustfully forward, unaware of the conflicting political interests that would make her the pawn in a game of selfish ambitions. Her uncle knew well that his reunion with the daughter of King Louis XVI would enhance his position with the royalists, while the emperor of Austria felt that the marriage of an Austrian archduke with Madame Royale would add to Austria's prestige, ultimately secure rights to French provinces, and strengthen Austria's hand.

In the course of her journey she took time to write to Mme de Chantereine:

> *My dear little Rennette:—I still love you very much, and I am beginning my letter high on the page, against your teaching, so as to be able to get it fuller... I was recognized on the very first day at Provins. Oh, Rennette, how it hurt, and yet it was a joy! You cannot imagine how the people flocked to see me. Some called me their good lady, others their good Princess. They wept for joy, and I very nearly did so myself, my poor heart was profoundly agitated and mourned even more deeply the fatherland it still loves. What a difference between Paris and the departements! After Charenton no more* assignats *were accepted. There were loud murmurs against the Government, and the old masters were called for, even poor unhappy me! Every one deplores my departure. I am known everywhere, in spite of the efforts of those who accompany me. My sorrow increases at abandoning my unfortunate compatriots. Oh, my dear Rennette! If you only knew how touched I am! What a pity this change of feeling did not occur earlier! I should not then have witnessed the destruction of my whole family and of so many innocent victims. But enough of a subject which wounds me deeply . . .*
> *[Mémoires of Vicomte De Larochefoucauld,* IV Paris, 1837]

And then, in a different mood, "*There is a rumor that I am to be married to my lover—but it shall not be so—at any rate, for a long time.*" But later, with touching bewilderment, "*They talk so much of my marriage; they say it is to be soon. I hope not—at least, I do not know what I hope.*"

She took leave of her companions at the frontier and arrived in Vienna on January 9, 1796, where every attempt was made to alienate her from her French relatives. The Austrian emperor pressed her for her consent to marry his younger brother, Archduke Charles Louis. This she refused to do. Great pressure was brought to bear with this as well as other suggestions contrary to the young girl's wishes. She was later to write: "I was sent for by the Emperor's cabinet, where I found the imperial family assembled. The ministers and chief imperial counsellors were also present. . . . When the Emperor invited me to express my opinion, I answered that to be able to treat fittingly of such interests, I thought I ought to be surrounded not only by my mother's relatives, but also by those of my father. . . . Besides, I said, I was above all things *French*, and in entire subjection to the laws of France, which had rendered me alternately the subject of the King my father, the King my brother, and the King my uncle, and that I would yield obedience to the latter, whatever might be his command. This declaration appeared very much to dissatisfy all who were present, and when they observed I was not to be shaken, they declared that my right being independent of my will, my resistance would not be the slightest obstacle to the measures they might deem it necessary to adopt for the preservation of my interests."

After this Madame Royale was so closely watched

and held under such check that, though in a more luxurious way, she was again a prisoner.

M. Huë, in his loyalty, had followed Madame Royale to Vienna and was the secret go-between in correspondence of the King and his niece, although he had been forbidden to see her. He gave her instructions as to how she might communicate with her uncle, advising her to use lemon juice to conceal her writing. Part of this advice was: "I will go to the ramparts on Monday about half-past twelve, and shall be there each day until Madame is able to signify her wishes to me. If Madame consents to use lemon, will she kindly blow her nose several times? If I touch my ear with my hand, it will indicate that I have understood her sign. When I have a letter from the King for Madame, I will take it to Madame de C [Chanclos] conformably to instructions. I will then go to the ramparts, and if I play with Coco it will be a sure sign that I have delivered the letter to her." [Baron de Maricourt, *Souvenirs de M. Huë*]

Madame Royale must have taken advantage of M. Huë's elaborate procedure for, in a letter to Louis XVIII she felt desperate enough to write, "I am much touched by your kindness in seeking to arrange a marriage for me. As you have selected the Duc d'Angoulême for my husband, I consent with all my heart . . . I joyfully accept my cousin d'Angoulême; your choice could not have fallen on any man more agreeable to me. I hope the marriage will soon take place."

Finding no success in obtaining his niece's release by other means, in 1798 Louis petitioned the then sympathetic Czar Paul to use his influence with the court of Vienna to permit Madame Royale to live with whom she chose—namely, to join him.

"Madame Royale shall be restored to you or I shall cease to be Paul I," was the answer, and the next day the czar sent a message to Vienna so strongly worded that it might have been interpreted as a threat of war. This produced the desired results. Without further ado Madame Royale was handed over to what remained of the French royal family.

In an old ducal castle in Russia a pathetic little group of exiles awaited the daughter of Louis XVI and Marie Antoinette. It consisted of Louis XVIII, his wife, their nephews the Duc d'Angoulême and the Duc de Berri, the Comte d'Artois, Abbé Edgeworth who had accompanied her father to the scaffold, and a small party of emigrant nobles and officers. These, together with a man by the name of De Malden, who had acted as a courier to her father during the flight to Varennes, and Turgi, who had waited on Madame Royale and her aunt in the Temple, now comprised the Court of France.

On June 10, 1799, Madame Royale was married to her cousin, the Duc d'Angoulême—a marriage founded not on romantic inclination but on family policy and on Madame Royale's desire to fulfill what she thought would have been the wishes of her parents. Her first sight of the cousin she remembered as a child was a shock. He was scarcely any taller now than then and he was frail and sickly in appearance. His face was ugly and he suffered from defective eyesight. All in all, he was not the Prince Charming she may have dreamed of. Another dream would not be realized—they would never have children.

In January, 1801, Czar Paul, yielding to the demand of Napoleon, ordered the royal family to leave Russia. Their wanderings started on the twenty-first, on order of immediate expulsion. Hard pressed for money, Marie Thérèse offered her heirloom diamonds to the Danish consul, saying she pledged her jewels "that in our common distress it may be rendered of real use to my uncle, his faithful servants, and myself."

They traveled to Warsaw where they again risked expulsion following the attempts of Napoleon to bribe or threaten Louis XVIII into abdication and the forfeit of his claim. The King's answer was, "We are accustomed to suffering, and we do not dread poverty. I would, trusting in God, seek another asylum."

They did "seek another asylum," this time in England. An annual grant of twenty-four thousand pounds was made to the exiled family by the sympathetic British government and they moved to Hartwell Hall, a fine old Elizabethan mansion which they were able to rent for about five hundred pounds a year. In April, 1814, however, enthused by the royalists' successes at Bordeaux after Napoleon's fall and by the good wishes of their English friends, including the Prince Regent himself, they set out for France to restore the Bourbon monarchy.

In May the royal family were again ensconced in the Tuileries, a place of tearful memories, and there they maintained a lackluster sort of court. Marie Thérèse was successful in having what were identified as her parents' remains removed from the cemetery of the Madeleine where they had been thrown and, in an impressive ceremony, interred in the Abbey of St. Denis, the traditional burial place of the kings of France.

But the fate of the Bourbons continued to fluctuate, attuned to the erratic changes of the government of France. Napoleon's escape from Elba in February, 1815, threw the royalists into a panic and the royal family fled in all directions.

The king hastily withdrew from Paris; Marie Thérèse's father-in-law the Comte d'Artois, together with his immediate family, retreated from the frontier; and her husband the Duc d'Angoulême, who had been made head of the royalist troops, set sail on a Swedish ship for Spain.

Marie Thérèse, and Marie Thérèse alone, took a stand against the general alarm. Refusing to leave Bordeaux, she mounted her horse and reviewed her own regiment. She made a passionate appeal to the remaining handful of officers and soldiers to hold fast, even when cannon fire from the opposite side of the river was directed towards the square where she had taken her stand. She was finally persuaded that her resistance was in vain, and soon Napoleon's banner triumphantly waved over Bordeaux. Napoleon himself, touched by the spirit of this royal princess, said: "She is the only man in the family," an observation strangely reminiscent of one that Honoré de Mirabeau, early leader of the French Revolution, had made about her mother, Marie Antoinette: "She is the only man whom his Majesty has about him."

So Marie Thérèse bade her "brave Bordelais" farewell and embarked, appropriately enough, on the British sloop *Wanderer* to join her husband in Spain. But, during a brief stop in England, news came of the end of Napoleon's "Hundred Days" and once more she returned to France where her uncle resumed his reign.

In September, 1824, Louis XVIII died and the Comte d'Artois, as the last remaining brother, took his oath as King Charles X. The French people were cold to this. There had been some respect for Louis; there was none for dissolute Charles. His ill-advised actions brought about such feeling against him that in 1830 he was forced to abdicate, and once more the Bourbons were obliged to flee to safety. Arriving at Cherbourg, they sailed for England.

The historic castle of Holyrood in Scotland was made available to the royal refugees, but before very long the French government nervously complained that they were too close to their native land. So they had to leave Edinburgh. Journeying by different routes, these survivors of a once powerful royal family met in Prague and from there moved from one place to another throughout the years.

In 1836 the ailing Charles X decided to spend the winter at Goritz near Trieste where the climate was said to be milder. He died there on November 6, leaving a fortune to be divided among his heirs. Now Marie Thérèse had at least financial security, but years of uncertainty had made her cautious enough even now to keep a little cache of jewels always close at hand "for emergencies."

The living style of both Marie Thérèse and her husband was simple. They rose at six in the morning, attended daily Mass, and were fond of the pleasures of walking, riding and reading together. They had become almost inseparable, but they had interests of their own. Studying the weather became a passion with him and she became involved in gardening, which unfortunately led to her husband's death. Joining her in her hobby one day, he cut himself. The cut became infected and he died of blood poisoning on June 3, 1844. They had been married for forty-five years. Theirs had not been a marriage of love but almost half a century of exile and suffering had made them tolerant and close; in late years companionship had ripened into tender affection. Now Marie Thérèse was alone.

In spite of her wanderings she had never ceased to love the land of her birth. But she was the daughter of a king and queen of France and she would never return while that country flew the tricolor national banner.

Perhaps in her sorrow her mind turned to the happy scenes of her childhood, and possibly the pastoral charm of a little town called Frohsdorf (about thirty miles from Vienna, her mother's native home) reminded her of the carefree days of the Petit Trianon. For it was there she settled, and it was there her wanderings came to an end. She died on October 19, 1851, at the age of almost seventy-three.

Carved into her tombstone, in Latin, are these words:

"Ask yourselves, all ye who pause here,
if your sorrows are equal unto mine."

CHRONOLOGICAL SUMMARY

April 21, 1770: The Dauphiness leaves Austria for France.

May 16, 1770: The Dauphin and Dauphiness are married in the chapel at Versailles.

1770-1774: The Dauphiness is caught up in the mad whirl of a teenage Court.

May 10, 1774: The Dauphin and Dauphiness become King Louis XVI and Queen Marie Antoinette.

December 19, 1778: A daughter, Marie Thérèse Charlotte, Madame Royale, is born.

October 22, 1781: First Dauphin, Louis Joseph Xavier, is born.

March 27, 1785: Second son, Louis Charles, is born.

August 15, 1785: National bankruptcy, and Cardinal de Rohan's arrest in the Diamond Necklace Scandal.

May 31, 1786: Acquittal of Cardinal de Rohan and the public turns against the Queen.

July 9, 1786: Daughter Sophie Béatrix is born. She dies at eleven months of age.

August 8, 1788: Summoning of States-General.

May 5, 1789: Opening of States-General.

June 3, 1789: Death of the Dauphin.

June 17, 1789: The Third Estate, the Commons, declares itself the National Assembly and refuses to dissolve.

June 20, 1789: The National Assembly takes the Oath of the Tennis Court.

July 11, 1789: Finance Minister Necker, friend of the people, is dismissed and banished.

July 13, 1789: Creation of the National Guard under the Marquis de La Fayette.

July 14, 1789: The storming of the Bastille.

July 15, 1789: The King calls up his troops.

July 17, 1789: The King goes to Paris to calm the people.

October 5, 1789: The people's march on Versailles following the "Insurrection of Women."

October 6, 1789: The Royal Family is taken to Paris.

October, 1789-June, 1791: Life in the Tuileries.

June 20-25, 1791: The flight to Varennes.

September 14, 1791: The King swears loyalty to the newly formed constitution and accepts constitutional monarchy.

April 20, 1792: France declares war on Austria.

June 19, 1792: The King exercises his right of veto, refusing to sanction the order for deportation of priests.

June 20, 1792: Riot and invasion of the Tuileries.

August 10, 1792: Attack on the Tuileries.

August 10-13, 1792: The Royal Family goes to the Assembly for protection.

August 13, 1792: The Royal Family is taken to the Temple.

September 2-5, 1792: The September Massacres and Princess de Lamballe's death.

December 11, 1792: Trial of the King.

January 21, 1793: Death of the King.

July 3, 1793: The little King is taken away.

August 2, 1793: The Queen is taken to the Conciergerie.

October 8, 1793: Madame Royale and Princess Elisabeth are interrogated.

October 12-14, 1793: Trial of the Queen.

October 16, 1793: Death of the Queen.

May 9, 1794: Trial of Princess Elisabeth.

May 10, 1794: Death of Princess Elisabeth.

May, 1794-June, 1795: Madame Royale alone.

June 8, 1795: Announcement of the little King's death.

June 22, 1795: A companion for Madame Royale.

September, 1795: Madame Royale is allowed visitors and gets the devastating news that her mother and aunt are dead.

December 19, 1795: Madame Royale is released from prison and leaves for Austria.

June, 1799-1851: Madame Royale becomes a bride, returns to Paris in triumph, becomes a crusader and a refugee.

October 19, 1851: Madame Royale's wanderings come to an end.

BIOGRAPHIES

Madame Royale: Marie Thérèse Charlotte, traditional title Madame Royale, daughter of King Louis XVI and Queen Marie Antoinette of France. Born December 19, 1778. Became Duchess d'Angoulême on marriage, June 10, 1799. Died in exile on October 19, 1851.

Louis XVI, King of France: Father of Madame Royale. Born August 23, 1754. Became king in 1774. After abolishment of monarchy, imprisoned, tried for treason, and executed January 21, 1793.

Marie Antoinette, Queen of France: Mother of Madame Royale. Born November 2, 1755. Daughter of Empress Maria Theresa of Austria. Married Louis, Dauphin of France in 1770. Imprisoned, tried, and guillotined October 16, 1793.

Louis Charles, Dauphin of France: Brother of Madame Royale. Born March 27, 1785. King at age 8, on death of father. Imprisoned with family; unsubstantiated report of death on June 8, 1795, gave rise to doubts. Later claimants to being Louis Charles not acknowledged.

Elisabeth of France: Aunt of Madame Royale, Princess Elisabeth, youngest sister of Louis XVI. Born 1764. Devoted to the royal family, especially her niece. Imprisoned with them and condemned to death. Guillotined on May 19, 1794.

Louis XVIII, King of France: Uncle of Madame Royale, the Comte de Provence. Born 1755, elder of two brothers of Louis XVI. On restoration of the Bourbon throne reigned 1814-15 and again 1815-24. Died September 16, 1824.

Charles X, King of France: Uncle of Madame Royale, the Comte d'Artois. Born 1756, younger brother of Louis XVI. Succeeded brother, Louis XVIII, in 1824; forced to abdicate and flee the country in 1830. Died in exile November 6, 1836.

Duc d'Angoulême: Husband of Madame Royale, Louis Antoine. Born 1775 at Versailles, son of the Comte d'Artois. Loyal supporter of uncle, Louis XVIII, and father, Charles X, during their restoration to the Bourbon throne. Became last Dauphin of France as elder son of Charles X. Renounced that title to live last years in quiet exile. Died in 1844.

Princess de Lamballe: Closest friend of the queen and appointed superintendent of the royal household. Born 1749. Voluntarily accompanied the royal family to imprisonment. Refused to subscribe to oath against monarchy; torn to pieces by enraged mob, September 3, 1792.

Marquise de Tourzel: Governess to Madame Royale and the Dauphin. Born 1750. Refused to abandon royal charges; was imprisoned with her own daughter. Asked to be confined with Madame Royale in the Temple. After Madame Royale's release retired to Abondant chateau; erected small monument in memory of royal family. Died in 1832.

Madame Campan: First Lady of the Bedchamber to Marie Antoinette. Born 1752. Following fall of king and queen, went into hiding until Reign of Terror ended. In 1794 opened girls' school; in 1807 appointed by Napoleon to head academy for female members of Legion of Honor families. In 1822 wrote her *Mémoirs of Marie Antoinette.* Died in 1822.

Marquis de La Fayette: Nobleman and patriot. Born 1757. Joined American Revolution at age 19; became protégé of General George Washington. Fought for French liberty but sought to preserve constitutional monarchy. Headed France's National Guard at inception and again in 1830 revolution at age 73. Died in 1834.

BIBLIOGRAPHY AND FURTHER READING LIST

As Told by the Duchess d'Angoulême, Madame Elisabeth, Sister of Louis XVI, and Cléry, the King's Valet de Chambre. Translated by Katharine Prescott Wormeley: *The Ruin of a Princess,* Lamb Publishing Co., New York, 1912.

Campan, Madame: *Mémoirs of the Court of Marie Antoinette and Anecdotes of her Private Life,* P. F. Collier & Son, New York, 1910.

Carlyle, Thomas: *The French Revolution,* Bennett A. Cerf, Donald S. Klopper, New York, 1934.

Castelot, André: *Queen of France,* Harper & Brothers, New York, 1957.

Holt, Victoria: *The Queen's Confession,* Doubleday & Company, Inc., Garden City, New York, 1968.

Huisman, Philippe and Jallut, Marguerite: *Marie Antoinette,* Translated by Edita Lausanne, The Viking Press, Inc., New York, 1971.

Latzko, Andreas. Translated by E.W. Dickes: *Lafayette, a Life,* Doubleday, Doran and Company, Inc., New York, 1936.

Pernoud, Georges and Flaissier, Sabine. Translated by Richard Graves: *The French Revolution,* Martin Secker & Warburg, Ltd., London, 1960.